101 Ways

to

Screw

Up

Your Wedding Reception
(Without Really Trying!)

Rex De Jaager

© 2012 by Rex De Jaager

101 Ways to Screw Up Your Wedding Reception (Without Really Trying)

Rex De Jaager

www.101waystoscrewupyourweddingreception.com

Email:
rexpert@101waystoscrewupyourweddingreception.com

Cover design: Evelyn J Wagoner
Interior design: Evelyn J. Wagoner

ISBN 978-0-9854926-2-5
Printed in the United States of America

Dedication

To all the brides and grooms who trusted me
with one of the most important days of their lives.

I hope others gain insight as I share my experiences.

Contents

Your Wedding Day

A Dream Come True . . .

or a Nightmare?

For your wedding day to be the triumphant occasion you've planned so carefully and thoughtfully, it must run smoothly. Like a well-oiled machine, each part must do its job. Just one gear out of place can upset the total process. Imagine if the officiate is late to the ceremony. Not only would that cause stress, it would also put a kink in the rest of the day. Most receptions are a delicate timeline of events. From the moment the alarm rings that morning, all the wheels that were put in place weeks (and sometimes months) ago begin to turn.

Let me tell you a story of how a wedding day *could* play out. I say *could*, because all of these situations have actually happened—though, I will admit, not all in one wedding. But, just for fun—and your edification—come along with me, and thank heavens you can avoid these pitfalls, because you were smart enough to buy this little book!

1

Imagine Mom making breakfast, perhaps for many more people than usual, as family has come in from out of town, and she has insisted that they all get together for a big, wedding morning feast. The bride's sister, one of the bridesmaids, is already stressing because she somehow got a spot on her dress. Dad is taking care of the dogs and making room in the driveway for the limo.

Meanwhile, the bride's hairdresser Shelley is having a hard time waking up. She stayed out too late partying the night before, but she's confident she'll be fine after a few cups of coffee. She'll just be a little jittery.

The baker is looking over her to-do list. It's a fairly light day with only three wedding cakes to deliver. However, two are needed at about the same time—and one happens to be our bride's. But she's not worried; she's done this before.

Uncle Bob still hasn't picked up his tux. He promised he would be there at 9:30 when the shop opens. (He hopes it will fit, as he's put on a couple of pounds since the last fitting.)

The florist has no concerns; she's handled hundreds of weddings. But who could have foreseen that the arch would fall over and crush the bridesmaids' bouquets? No problem! She can have new ones made in just forty-five minutes. The leftover flowers from yesterday's wedding will have to do even if the colors are a little off.

The organist pops a couple of painkillers so that the arthritis in her fingers will be a bit more tolerable. She'll be ready to go by one o'clock when the ceremony begins. Or is that noon? Better check again.

The weatherman says the skies will clear after last night's storm. The only remnant will be winds gusting at times from 15 to 20 miles per hour. Again, no problem. Just use a little more hairspray. And Dad will put an extra rock on the "Congratulations" sign at the end of the driveway, so it won't blow over.

The food director at the venue is already barking orders to the staff.

"Why wasn't this chicken defrosted last night?" she asks. "Are the champagne bottles in the cooler? They aren't? Get it done!"

She gives an order to add an extra table for eight, because she's been notified that some guests sent in RSVPs at the last minute.

"Move the DJ table to the other side of the dance floor. Put it next to the bar," she says. "I know it's going to be tight."

The chef has had two cups of coffee and three cigarettes. He's certain all his ducks are in a row. Other than the chicken (which hasn't quite defrosted), everything is on track for a perfect meal. He makes a quick phone call to make sure his assistant hasn't overslept again. Hopefully, he doesn't have to bail him out of jail like he did a month ago.

Dad calls the limo company to confirm the car's on the way. The woman who answers the phone tells him that Pedro the driver had just called for more detailed directions. Was that the second left or left at the fork? He'll be a few minutes later than planned; the pump at the gas station was pumping a bit slow, and it's a huge tank.

DJ Frank is pulling the baby seat out of his minivan to make room for his equipment. He brushes the seat to dislodge some of the dog hairs, so they don't stick to his speakers. Unlike past events, he's getting ready fifteen minutes earlier, because he's never done a gig at this particular venue. Frank wipes the CD his father gave him on his belly in small, circular motions to wipe off fingerprints and smudges. He slides it in the van's CD player to verify it's the song the bride wanted as a first dance song. It's a good thing Dad had the song in his oldies collection. A few notes into the song, he ejects it with the confidence it will work just fine. He replaces it with the CD his friend down the street gave him to try out. It has some cool tunes downloaded off the Internet. He smiles when he hears the great beat, then his expression changes when the singer lets loose a "#&$@*"! He'll have to remember to blank out the obscenities before he loads the CD at the reception.

When Frank pulls into a parking space in front of the cleaners, he's perplexed to see a closed sign hanging in the door. Closed? How can they be closed? The sign says there was a family emergency. But he needs that shirt! Well, hopefully the one in the backseat under the speaker doesn't have too much dog hair on it. Certainly, no one will notice. He spends most of the time behind his DJ rig anyway. It will have to do.

All the bride's attendants, except Betty, show up at the hair salon on time. She calls and says her babysitter is sick and can't watch little Patty. Can she bring her along?

Everyone looks at each other in horror and thinks, *Oh no! Not the A.D.D. cyclone!* Shelley the hairdresser produces a bottle of champagne, and tiny bubbles abound as everyone's hair is transformed into synchronized styles. Shelley reminds her staff to go heavy on the hairspray, remembering the forecast of gusting wind.

And then the photographer arrives.

"Hello, ladies. My name is Steve. I'm your photographer today. I thought I'd stop by and take a few candid shots of the bridal party getting ready."

Betty strolls in with little Patty, who runs and grabs a bottle of champagne from the bucket.

"Look, Mama! It's just like yours!"

Betty blushes and says under her breath, "Mother's little helper . . ."

Meanwhile, Heather, the catering director, inspects the reception room and barks out half a dozen orders to take care of details. She takes pride in making sure every little thing is just right.

"Why hasn't that bulb been replaced?

"Get that mess vacuumed up!"

"She paid for mirrored centerpieces. Go in the back, wipe off the mirrors, and set them at each table."

"Why are these flowers different colors?"

"Where's the DJ? Why hasn't he started setting up?"

"Did the chef get the message about the extra eight people?"

In the limo, the bride and her bridesmaids are on their way to the church, and the conversation goes something like this:

"Pedro, can you find a place for us to pee? That champagne is kicking in!"

"Betty, get yourself back in the limo. Pedro says we can't stand up through the sunroof, and it will mess up your hair!"

Betty plops down into her seat and says, "Wow! I'm buzzin' already."

"Ladies, pull yourselves together! We're almost at the church."

The organist's fingers are limber, and beautiful music is echoing off the walls and stained glass windows. The scent from the flower arrangements lingers throughout the sanctuary. Grandma is already weeping, and Grandpa is eyeballing one of the bridesmaids. Dad is a nervous wreck. The officiate is on time but has a pungent odor of perspiration. He pronounces the names correctly but forgets the bride and groom planned to say personal vows in addition to the traditional ones. A little juggling and a sidestep, and the vows are spoken. Part one is almost over with no major hiccups—other than Betty having to sit because she's too dizzy to stand and Patty shredding two of the pew flower arrangements.

And then the officiate announces, "Ladies and gentlemen, I'm proud to present Mr. and Mrs. ... " Again, at least he pronounces the names correctly.

Now it's photo time. Steve jumps in and begins

orchestrating a traditional sequence directing the wedding party, the parents, then just the bride and groom to stand here and there, as he snaps the photos that will find their way onto the coffee table or the fireplace mantel. It's a shame Betty won't be in most of them, since she's spending a little quality time with the porcelain god.

Back at the reception venue, it's thirty minutes to "show time," and Frank the DJ has finally arrived. The front-desk receptionist tells him he can't carry his equipment through the main entrance and has to drive around back to the loading dock. Heather, the catering director, gives Frank the "look of death," as she shows him where to set up. She's still busy finalizing details and is looking for someone with a lighter. "We need to get those candles lit NOW."

Frank didn't realize he would be so far from an outlet and asks if he can borrow an extension cord. Heather shakes her head and sighs. She's seen way too many so-called professionals of this caliber before. The guests are arriving, and Frank is still plugging in his last few wires. Without time to do sound checks, he runs around to the back of his rig and grabs the first jazz CD he finds. He again rubs it on his belly, as if it were a good-luck gesture. Tossing it into the CD player, he presses play and then jogs outside to his mini-van. There, he grabs his wrinkled shirt from the backseat (yes, it has dog hair on it) and runs to the men's room to make himself at least somewhat more presentable.

Pedro is slightly behind schedule because he had to stop twice to allow Betty a closer look at the roadside. The eyes of the older Mrs. Smith meet the eyes of the new Mrs.

Smith. The new Mrs. Smith interprets the look as, *"This is all your fault."* But, in the back of her mind, the older Mrs. Smith is actually thinking, *What has my son gotten himself into?*

The guests are relieved to see the bridal party has finally arrived, signifying that the reception can officially begin. Frank approaches the new Mr. and Mrs. Smith. His first words are an apology for not having met with them last week, but he reassures them he did receive their e-mail and will do his best. He rushes back to his station to begin the music and the grand entrance in which he only butchers two names.

On a good note, the first dance is well on its way... until the last few moments of the song. It seems someone left a juicy thumbprint on the CD and, suddenly, it begins skipping, turning the newly-married couple's memorable first dance into something sounding like a digital remix. The bride and groom find their way to the sweetheart table and look at each other, shaking their heads with disgust, as Frank pulls the CD from the player looking at it with a puzzled expression.

A few minutes later, Frank loads his well-worn Kenny G CD for the dinner background music. Heather jumps into action and begins delegating to the staff. No announcement was made regarding the meal, so the guests have no idea what to expect as the caterer's assistants begin serving salads.

Patty, the A.D.D. cyclone, finds this an opportune moment to sample the cake. She looks left, then right, and, with a finger, takes a big swipe at the base of the cake. Unfortunately for her, Grandma was looking her way.

Grandma tugs on Betty's dress and tells her to control her child. So Betty yells across the room, "Patty! Get your ass over here!" The whole room falls silent as they catch sight of Patty with her finger halfway to her mouth. The conversations slowly resume. Patty thinks she'd better hide, so she crawls under Frank's table. She doesn't stay very long after catching a couple of sniffs of what looks like a gym bag filled with dirty laundry.

Heather approaches Mr. and Mrs. Smith and apologizes for the delay on the meal. She says the chicken is almost done and should be ready to plate and serve soon. Mrs. Smith turns to her husband and rolls her eyes. What time is it? Are they going to have time to dance? Everyone had advised her to have at least a four-hour reception, but three hours was more in the budget. Mrs. Smith decides to ask Frank to do the parents' dances now to save time later. She looks over to the table hiding the gym bag and supporting a gaggle of home-stereo equipment, but Frank isn't there. Heather passes by with the first meals, so the bride asks her if she has seen the DJ. The catering director responds, "The last time I saw him, he was outside smoking with half of the bridal party."

Uncle Bob takes it upon himself to open the outside door and announce, "Hey, DJ, your music stopped in here." Frank rushes in to discover that someone has unplugged his system under the table. He plugs it back in and re-starts the Kenny G.

The bride and groom have just taken their second bites when the photographer approaches and says this would be a great time to take a couple of photos outside near the entrance. They take one more bite and make a beeline toward the door. This gives a dozen people the opportunity to stand and congratulate them. The journey to the front door now takes about ten minutes. During this time, Steve makes his way to Frank's haven and asks him to make an announcement. After a short squeal from the feedback and a few taps on the mike, Frank says, "Yo, listen up, folks! The photographer wants the bridal party outside for a picture."

Heather looks up from serving another plate in horror, thinking, *This can't be! We're serving the meal!* She hurries over to Steve just as he's about to exit and questions his timing. He uses the excuse that Mr. and Mrs. Smith requested these photos. What he doesn't tell her is that the request came weeks ago during their first consult and that he hadn't spoken with the couple since then. He reassures her they will return in five minutes.

Jack, a guest and part-time DJ at a local club, makes his way to Frank's stand

"Hey, dude! What are you doing? Are you going to play Kenny G all night? My girlfriend—she's the one with the cool tattoo on her back—she's threatening to shoot herself if you don't play something she can dance to—and you should see her dance! C'mon, change it up a little, man!"

Frank grabs the first CD he touches. After the ceremonious belly rub, he throws it in the tray. Moments later, his neighbor Fred's CD is entertaining the guests.

About fifteen minutes later, Mr. and Mrs. Smith come back into the reception hall just in time to hear "#&$@*" blast from the speakers.

Oh, no! I forgot about Fred's CD, Frank thinks in

horror—though he isn't nearly as horrified as the bride, her mother, or several other guests. He hurriedly presses "stop" and looks up to see everyone staring at him in shock. He holds up a hand in apology, then quickly grabs another random CD. Seconds later, greatest hits from the disco era begin playing.

Mr. and Mrs. Smith return to their seats to find their meals are cold. Patty and a dozen of her closest new friends are running around, screaming, and spinning donuts on the dance floor.

After the parents dance, Heather asks the new Mrs. Smith if she would like to do the cake cutting now since there are only forty-five minutes left. Tears gather in the bride's eyes, and she blinks rapidly to try to ward them off.

Frank has progressed in just a few songs to full-blown 90s hip-hop.

"Becky, have you seen her butt? She looks like one of those rap guy's girlfriends."

Jack, his tattooed girlfriend, and the donut spinners are the only guests on the dance floor, while Mr. and Mrs. Smith prepare for the toast and cake cutting. Frank cuts the music abruptly and makes the announcement that the toast is about to take place. He doesn't have a cordless microphone, so he runs his fifty-foot cord across the floor to the cake table.

Dead air continues as the Best Man removes a two-page manifesto from his vest pocket. He begins with the disclaimer that he's had a few drinks but will do the best he can. He reads . . . and reads. There's something about how he will miss picking up girls at the bar with Mr. Smith and taking them back to his apartment. He adds a few Internet jokes about Mr. Smith placing his hand upon hers and how that will be the last time he has the upper hand, and then finally the toast. Mrs. Smith's Matron of Honor has planned a speech too but decides after hearing the first one that she'll just say a couple of words and put it to rest.

Heather the caterer and Steve the photographer at least seem to be on the same team as they direct Mr. and Mrs. Smith to the cake. But Mr. and Mrs. Smith are one of those couples who decides to redistribute their lovely cake into a couple of nasal passages. Frank fires up the music again, while Mr. and Mrs. Smith clean up.

Steve strikes up a conversation with a bridesmaid he finds interesting. He compliments the tattoos on her back. She then divulges that she has a few more but cannot display them in public. He talks her into letting him take a few "off the record" pictures—after all, he is a professional photographer. They skip out the side door looking for somewhere secluded for the private shoot. Some of those photos are most likely now on the Internet.

Mrs. Smith excitedly grabs the hand of her Matron of Honor and drags her towards the dance floor. But she notices that half the guests are heading towards the door. Mr. Smith is doing shots at the bar with his buddies. Mom is busy saying goodbye to her friends. Patty and her posse have made a fort under the cake table, and kids are crawling in and out. Though guests are still in the room, Frank decides to shut down his music and begin loading up his equipment. Mr. Smith has his arms slung around the necks of his buddies and is being assisted out the door. He's slurring, "I'm ready to take off that garter!"

Mrs. Smith walks behind them, bouquet in hand, a

glum look on her face. She asks her mother to call her in the morning for the debriefing. She wasn't really sure she would want to talk about everything that went wrong and how embarrassed her mother was, but she might as well get it over with right away.

The staff begins to clean up, pulling linens from the tables, exposing dozens of champagne glasses under the cake table and an empty pint of vodka under the DJ table. Steve walks in with his newest friend in tow and asks, "What happened? Where did they go?"

Sound outlandish? Sadly, it isn't. All of these incidents actually have happened. (The names, of course, have been changed to protect the unprofessional and those who would be embarrassed and humiliated.)

The celebration is what it is, and all the planning or lack thereof will define it. One always hopes for the best, but a wedding reception should not be left up to luck or to those individuals who call themselves professionals but who provide services that are not.

True professionals can make or break your event. When I say "true," I don't mean those that claim to be or those that have some verbiage on a tri-fold brochure that claims they are. Do the homework. Visit your professionals in person. Ask them questions. Ask for referrals—then contact those referrals to be sure they're legitimate. Ask the venues about the vendors. Ask the vendors about the venues. Ask to taste the food. Ask to taste the cake.

Demand to meet the DJ who will perform at the event. Notice that I used the word "perform." Your DJ does more than play CDs. Your DJ should have a great personality and be good with people, as he is the liaison between you and your guests. Make sure you like him! Ask to see in person (or have a video) of the band you are interested in.

Plan for all possible circumstances. Don't just have a Plan A . . . have a Plan B. Don't believe everything you hear from the professionals and vendors you choose. Check facts on your own. Make sure they can deliver what they promise.

That's right; it's so easy for a vendor to create an environment of grandeur beforehand about how easy it will be to take this picture and that. What isn't said is the level of coordination a photographer needs to have with all other professionals. Sadly many have their own agendas. You'll have to trust me when I tell you, it's not because they want to artistically create the best photo moment to end up in a local magazine but rather to sell you and your family more 8x10s. Discuss in full detail with your photographer about what is going to happen and when so *you* have control over the environment.

Go Ahead—
Make It Your Day!

How This Book Can Save Your Reception and Make It Truly an Event to Remember . . . with a Smile

The moment has finally arrived. You hold your beautiful bouquet in front of you, take the arm of your dad—your stepfather, brother, or whoever is honored with the privilege of walking you down the aisle—and give the nod. You're ready. The music you've so carefully chosen begins to play, and you step into the spotlight. Every eye is on you—the bride—floating down the aisle towards the love of your life—just as you'd always dreamed . . . or at least as close to it as you can afford.

Take a look at almost any bridal magazine or book on wedding planning, and you'll read that most brides began dreaming of their wedding day when they were just little girls. And it's true. I've asked bride after bride, and almost all remember playing wedding day with their Barbie dolls.

15

Give a little boy a dishtowel or a pillowcase, and it becomes a superhero's cape. Give a little girl the same thing and, more often than not, it becomes a bridal veil.

Is that day soon to become a reality for you? What dreams have you held dear for your wedding? What have you imagined? A sequined, flowing white gown with a long train? A smart, modern-mini with a stylish hat and short veil? A bouquet of daisies, roses, or calla lilies? Bach's *Ode to Joy? Freebird? Bless the Broken Road?* Being waltzed romantically (or jitterbugging?) around the dance floor by your own Prince Charming, while the adorable flower girl and ring bearer follow your lead? What? *Follow your lead?* Yep. You've stumbled upon a key reality.

Your guests will, indeed, follow your lead. If you dance, they will dance. If you are a smoker and spend time outside smoking, so will your guests. It's your party. Each of your guests knows it's your party, and they'll look to you to set the tone. If you're unhappy or disappointed for some reason, you won't be able to hide it. And your guests will reflect your attitude—they'll be uncomfortable, unsociable, and most likely head for the door at the earliest opportunity. Not exactly what you dreamed of, is it? So how do you avoid a wedding reception that, when you're looking back on it, makes you cringe instead of smile blissfully?

Well, for starters, you've picked up this little book. Good move. You won't be disappointed. ***101 Ways to Screw Up Your Wedding Reception (Without Really Trying!)*** is written by a professional who knows receptions inside and out—what works and what doesn't. With insight into potential problems and circumstances far too many brides have unwittingly encountered, the author can help you avoid unforeseen disasters.

Take heart! It's true—you actually *can* have the wedding reception of your dreams!

Plan A, Plan B . . .

Square One . . . Where to Begin

Every bride knows how much money she can afford to spend on her wedding, but very few know how to spend that money sensibly. Every *wise* bride will have that budget divided into how much she can spend on the individual aspects of her wedding: invitations, her dress, flowers, photographer, the ceremony (officiate, musicians, soloists, flowers, photographer), and the reception (venue/location, cake, caterer, decorations, DJ/band, etc.). Problems arise when the bride fails to consider important issues ahead of time.

#1 My parents are paying for the wedding and reception, so they want everything their way.

Yes, the person holding the purse strings usually has the power, but the wedding is supposed to be about the bride and groom (especially the bride!).

During one interview with a bride and groom, I was told the groom was a huge AC/DC fan and that he would like the couple to be introduced at the reception to one of their songs. The bride thought it was a great idea, and so we planned the grand introductions to their liking.

At the reception, just before I was about to begin the introductions, the mother of the bride scurried up to my booth and said, "No, no, no! We will not have that kind of music played at this event!"

When I respectfully reminded her that it was her daughter's reception and not hers, she then pulled the "I'm-paying-for-this-party" argument. I responded by telling her that I was willing to pull the plug if she thought it made a difference. The point was taken, and she backed off. Yes, she remained in a foul mood, but she apologized at the end of the event, when she realized that a mixture of music made the reception a success. And—best of all—her daughter and new son-in-law had a wonderful time.

It's important to find the happy medium between the purse strings and the bride and groom. Parents sometimes have a different perspective when it comes to how their money is spent and how they want to "entertain" (or impress) their friends. Did you notice the root of the problem? Yes, "their friends." Moms and dads are sometimes wrapped up in how the event is pulled together, because they are doing their best to impress their friends. So why are the friends even there? Because if Mom and Dad are going to fork over lots of money for a festive event, then they are going to take advantage of the occasion and invite a few close friends and, perhaps, business associates. Sometimes a bride and groom will tell you that only a fraction of the people in attendance were their close friends with the rest being invited by their parents. Although this may gain a few points for the parents, it doesn't always turn out to be the ideal event for the bride and groom. Imagine being in a room filled primarily with total strangers. Even though parents may pay the bill, they need to remember that the event is focused on the bride and groom. It is their day, and it is their dreams and desires that should be realized.

#2   The service personnel are upset; I've paid the bill, but I can't afford to tip anyone.

Gratuities are always expected in the service community. From limo drivers to bartenders, you must be prepared to tip those that serve you well. Your entertainers' gratuity should be based on performance and professionalism. When developing your budget, be sure to allocate adequate funds for gratuities.

#3   I spent $1000 on a cheese, vegetable, and fruit table for hors d'oeuvres, and it was barely touched.

One bride and groom splurged on an extravagant cheese, fruit, and vegetable tray. Actually, it turned out to be not a tray at all but an entire table! I was curious about the cost and was shocked to hear that it was $1000! Sixty-six people attended the wedding and most stayed for the entire evening. Photos taken of the hors d'oeuvres before and after the event proved to be very similar—evidence that hardly any of the elaborate spread was eaten. My question: Where could the money have been better spent? Not only that, but think of the waste! Trust me, the staff is tired of taking home dried-up cheese and picked-over vegetables. Most of it is simply thrown away.

Think of it this way. If an individual goes to a car lot

and sees a wide variety of cars, you might first consider why you need a new car. Do you need a minivan to transport kids and groceries, or do you only want a cool-looking sports car? How much will it cost to maintain that car? Insurance, gas, repairs, personal-property taxes? What's the sense in buying a Ferrari, if all you can do is park it in the garage because the insurance is too high? A wedding reception has a multitude of choices that will impact the entire event. Holding your event at the Ritz but only having enough money left to have an "iPod" playing music at your reception doesn't sound like smart planning. Hiring a national band like Nickelback to entertain would be great, but not so much if you only have enough money remaining to rent a VFW hall for the venue.

Ask yourself the important questions to help you decide your priorities. What things are more important to you? The dress or the entertainment? The food or the venue? How many people are invited or the type of flowers? A great deal of money will be spent on a very special day, and those choices will impact every part of the occasion. Work out a budget with all the choices balanced for the best celebratory event possible.

#4 I wish I would have spent my money on... something else.

It's a common lament. An extravagant event can be very expensive. Wouldn't it be great to know just where to spend the budget and how much to spend on each item? You can start by asking yourself good questions. For instance, which is more important for the success of your event: spending more money on the location or on quality food? Spending more on your dress or on the limo?

Spending more on flowers or on the DJ? Look at it this way. Some brides spend more on the shrimp cocktail than they do on the entertainment, then wonder why their guests left the reception early. Spend your money wisely and on the right things. These things may be different for each bride. Think things through thoroughly from start to finish.

#5 I wanted an early wedding, but I didn't realize my guests would go home so soon.

Many brides say they've dreamed of having a mid-afternoon wedding like they've seen in the movies. The weddings always look so romantic, and everyone seems to be having such a good time—but that's the Hollywood version. Afternoon weddings are fine, but in most cases guests are thinking about what they're going to do after the wedding. Many won't be drinking, because they don't typically imbibe that early in the day. Some will have already made plans for after the reception and will leave early to get started on those plans.

Brides who prefer a less stressful, "kicked-back" environment may find that an afternoon event is perfect for them. But bear in mind that I've observed that people don't always dance as much in an early afternoon setting. It could be because there is less consumption of alcohol or, again, because guests just aren't typically in high party mode at that time of day.

If you want a high-energy event with guests staying for several hours, an afternoon wedding may not be your best choice.

#6 I thought having my wedding during the Christmas season would be romantic. I was surprised to find out I was wrong.

A lot of wedding proposals take place during the Christmas season and, as a result, many couples plan to get married on or near the date of the proposal. In addition, with the lights, decorations, music, and overall loving spirit, the holiday season in itself is quite romantic. On the flipside, it's also the most stressful time of year. Adding a wedding and reception only multiplies the stress.

There are many factors working against you during the holidays. First, you're competing for venues with corporations booking holiday parties. Finding your perfect venue might prove to be difficult. If it is available, the price might be increased because of the competition. Second, you will also be competing for staff. If there are three other events scheduled at the same time, your reception may suffer from personnel stretched too thin. Wedding receptions are similar to family reunions, because so many family members arrive from so many different locations. Finding reasonable hotel accommodations during the holidays can be another difficulty. On the other hand, some family members prefer to celebrate the holidays at home and will decline the invitation to your wedding to avoid traveling during the hectic season.

Consider all these factors before deciding to hold your wedding during the holidays. If you choose to move ahead with your plans, get started as soon as possible. The earlier you book your venues and vendors, sign contracts, and put down deposits to confirm your arrangements, the more likely you'll have what you've dreamed of.

#7 I didn't know there would be a difference between having my wedding on Sunday and having it on Saturday.

Unless it's a three-day weekend, there most likely *will* be a difference. Many brides choose to get married on Sunday because of the difference in price. Yes, certain things may be less expensive, but it may not be worth the savings. Again, most people won't let their proverbial hair down to truly enjoy themselves on the day before they have to go back to work. Some will leave early, using the excuse that they have to get ready for the workweek. It's also difficult for some to arrive for an event from out of town and return home late Sunday when they have to work on Monday.

Given the choice between having your celebration on a Saturday versus a Sunday (or any other day for that matter), Saturday typically is the best choice for a successful event. That said, different people have different definitions of a successful event. If a quiet gathering with a small group of family and friends early in the afternoon is what you have in mind, then Sunday will work very well for you. Bottom line? A Saturday event may cost more, but, in most cases, the event has a better chance of being a success.

#8 I thought I could have my ceremony and reception in a four-hour block.

Many wedding ceremonies take an hour. This includes the half-hour while the guests are arriving and the twenty to thirty minutes for the ceremony itself. (If the ceremony is Catholic or Jewish, it will last closer to an hour.) A cocktail "hour" typically lasts only forty-five

24

minutes. Dinner, depending on the number of guests and how it is served, can take from forty-five minutes to an hour and a half. That's three hours. Toasts, cutting the cake, tossing the bouquet and garter, etc., take anywhere from twenty to thirty minutes. Do the math. That leaves just thirty minutes for dancing.

Most successful events are about four hours long. If you add in the wedding ceremony and the cocktail hour, I recommend stretching it to six hours. Receptions rarely last longer than that.

#9   Two people passed out at our ceremony.

A very nice couple held their ceremony on the grass at one of the local yacht clubs early one afternoon in the middle of June. The bride was a strict Indian Catholic, and the groom was Jewish. After a full Catholic mass and a traditional Jewish ceremony, ninety minutes had passed, and two guests passed out from the heat. When you're considering an outdoor ceremony, think about the weather and the time of year. Remember, it rains a lot in April, and July and August are horrendously hot. Have mercy on your guests . . . and on yourself.

#10 I thought my friends would have a blast if my wedding reception lasted until 2:00 a.m., just like when we're out at the nightclubs.

I see it all the time. A couple may have met, had some good times, or partied with friends at a local club. Now it's time to have the biggest party of their lives and invite those they've had fun with in the past. The only problem is that a reception venue is not a club, and not everyone invited wants to be up all night and part of the morning. Parents, grandparents, and most families prefer to retire before midnight. If your reception goes on too long—or if it devolves into a nightclub scene—most of your guests are likely to leave before you get to your romantic departure amidst the flurry of birdseed, bubbles, or whatever you plan for your guests to throw. Think about what is really important to you, and plan accordingly.

#11 I can't really have fun at my own reception, because I have to be up at 3:30 a.m. to go to the airport.

Time after time, I hear how the bride and groom are already stressed just anticipating the early departure the morning after their wedding to leave for their honeymoon. If the event ends at 10 or 11 p.m., we can assume the newly-married couples typically don't go directly to their honeymoon suites or homes and sleep. Some even meet with family and friends after receptions to continue celebrating. Before they know it, it's 2:00 a.m. and the wakeup call is in an hour. I always hear, "I'll sleep on the plane." Lack of sleep for 24 to 48 hours can make the beginning of the honeymoon tiring and listless. Postponing trips for a day or so will not only make your honeymoon more enjoyable, but you can visit with friends and family who came in from out of town and perhaps even have a morning-after celebratory brunch with all the VIPs.

#12 I didn't plan for overtime at my event.

What if you don't want the party to end? *Overtime* is another important factor to consider. What if everyone is having such a good time that you want the event to go on a little longer? You approach your entertainment to stay an extra hour but find that the venue cannot hold the staff any longer. How disappointing!

One of the most stressful things brides and grooms deal with the day of their wedding is clockwatching. Most brides don't even wear watches on their wedding day. It can add a great deal of tension if the newlyweds have to worry about the time and the fast-approaching end of the event. This can be less of a worry if you've planned ahead and asked the venue, as well as the other vendors, all the pertinent questions. Most have no problem extending the event for a fee, as long as there isn't an event immediately following yours.

So, when you book your venue and all vendors, including your entertainer, ask about overtime. Is there another function scheduled after yours? How much notice do you need? How much will it cost?

Location, Location, Location

What's Right for You?

So you want the perfect wedding. Every couple does—and everyone has his or her idea of what constitutes that perfect wedding. Is yours a tranquil church sanctuary filled with the scent of roses? Perhaps it's an outdoor wedding in a garden or on the beach. Or would you rather shout your vows mid-air after leaping from a perfectly good aircraft? There are as many different scenarios as there are brides and grooms. But the one thing they all have in common is that they want their guests to enjoy and feel comfortable at the wedding reception.

#13 I chose the wrong venue.

I've worked with millionaires who pinched every penny to the point where their guests, their close friends, and even their families felt the squeeze. One client tried hard to get the most for the least amount of money and whined about the expense of the large site. The suggestion

28

to instead use a local church venue was greeted with open arms. This bride had the means to afford the nicest venue in town but had the mindset that every penny was to be saved.

A few weeks later, we were discussing the particulars of the event. It was clear the bride was growing concerned that many of her guests might not attend because of the lack of glamour associated with what was expected to be the event of the season. Perhaps it sounds juvenile, but the truth is that your friends and family expect to be in surroundings they're familiar with. If your guests are used to using expensive, top-of-the-line golf clubs and wearing Dolce Cabana shoes, then they'll be expecting a "country-club" style reception with all the bells and whistles included.

There is a wide variety of venues ranging from clubs, churches, community centers, rental properties, lodges, and backyards to top-of-the-line venues with formal ballrooms. As there are no rental fees required, the absolute lowest end of the cost spectrum would be a social gathering in a home (living room or backyard) with a few select guests. Another lower cost option for a reception would be to invite your guests to a nightclub without any organized seating or attention. Of course the entertainment in this type of venue is completely subject to the whims of the bar or nightclub.

Still respectable, yet affordable, would be the smaller private venues, such as a VFW, Moose Lodge, Masonic Lodge, community center, or church social hall. Some can be decorated very nicely and at minimal expense. It is important to remember that someone has to do the actual decorating, feeding of the guests, and cleaning up. It is a lot of work, and you may prefer your family and friends to have a good time and not have to spend the entire reception—before, during, and after—working. One option is to hire someone to handle the extra details for you.

Vacation rentals are a popular option, especially in coastal towns. A large vacation rental can accommodate a large party and do double duty as accommodations for family and friends (and maybe even be used as the bridal suite).

Again, the environment you create for your special day will reflect back on you.

#14 I wasn't prepared for the unpredictable.

Many couples choose to have the reception close to home—maybe even in Mom and Dad's backyard. Depending on the variables, having your event outdoors can be dreamy—or an utter nightmare. While you would hope and pray for a beautiful day, you should have a "rain plan," just in case. Most professional catering and entertainment companies will not put their staff or their equipment in peril.

A tent is a good insurance blanket in case of rain. Depending on the time of year, a tent with flaps or walls can help protect your guests from rain, cold wind, or the hot summer sun.

I once worked with a bride on what would hopefully be a beautiful wedding in her uncle's backyard. Five acres of pristine grass were covered with a beautiful tent. Everything had been planned from the dance floor to convenient portable johns. But we couldn't have predicted the four days of rain prior to the event. After the crew had set up the tent, it was evident that the ground could not withstand the traffic. It was quickly becoming a huge field of mud.

While many solutions were discussed, the only cost-effective method that would absorb moisture and keep the ground intact was to use hay. Imagine the bride's disappointment. Her dream of an elegant event ended up looking more like a hoedown. Her friends and family still had a good time. Some guests had to use a little elbow grease in cleaning their shoes, and some clothing needed professional cleaning, but the event was still a success overall.

#15 This is my wedding—not a paid vacation for my guests!

Holding your event at a major landmark hotel or attraction can often detract from your event, as your guests may be more interested in viewing the attractions or visiting the five-star dining room than focusing on you and your special day. Although it seems first-class to be entertaining your guests at a memorable location, it may, in fact, backfire and draw all the attention away from your wedding. Some examples of this would be having your event at a museum that is having demonstrations during your event or at a water park or arcade. While children would definitely be entertained at the park's activities, their parents would have to be constantly chasing after the kids. Checking out the features, attractions, and amusements would be first on many guests' minds, and you would find yourself without the attention and company of the friends you've invited.

Also take into consideration the fact that decorating at some specialty venues could be difficult. Certain places, such as museums, may have policies restricting the use of decorations.

In addition, many specialty venues may be too large for a wedding reception with a minimal amount of people. A small wedding party can feel lost in a location that is too large—no matter how exciting, beautiful, or romantic it may be.

#16 There is nowhere to park.

Parking may not be a high priority at first glance, but depending on the number of guests and vehicles, it can easily become a major concern. In a tight residential area, it's unreasonable to expect your guests to walk several blocks—especially if many of those guests are wearing high heels. Some hotel venues also have limited parking space for unregistered guests, especially during peak seasons.

Some areas may have vacation homes that can be used for special events. Even so, the driveway will not accommodate all your guests' cars. Planning ahead and working with local stores, using large parking lots and mass transportation, such as limos, small buses, or vans can alleviate serious parking problems.

If you plan to be married on a military base, or if you're holding your reception at an officers club or at another on-base venue, be sure to check out all details in advance. Gaining access to military bases for your guests can be a challenge, unless you've done your homework. Vehicles may need to be searched; paperwork must be in order, and there can be long delays. Shuttle buses might be used to aid in the transport of guests. The same may be true for gated communities. Make sure you've worked out access for your guests in advance.

#17 Guests do not like paying for parking.

Is it okay to ask your guests to pay for parking to attend your reception? Some venues are located where the only parking available is paid or valet parking. In some cases, this can add up to a substantial amount for your guests to pay (sometimes as much as $20.00) or a significant amount if you are paying for your guests. Be sure to check with the venue to see if parking is validated or if exceptions are made.

#18 The location of the wedding ceremony/reception was too far from hotels and airports.

One gentleman confessed how much work it was to book every bed and breakfast in a ten-mile area to accommodate his guests. And then there were the hours upon hours of commutes to the airport to pick up relatives. It can be a logistical nightmare. Depending on the number of guests and the location of your event, you need to plan well for all situations. Destination events must have well-coordinated locations for guest arrivals (drop-off/pickup for elderly or disabled guests or in case of inclement weather), parking, and transportation needs (catering vans, band or DJ equipment loading, etc.).

Wedding receptions are, in part, family reunions. Families may want to get together before or after your event. Accommodations located over a large area make these gatherings inconvenient. Choose a central location for your out-of-town guests and family.

#19 We missed important moments, because our venue had too many rooms.

Venues that have two, three, and sometimes four rooms for a single event can be cause for confusion. If the entertainment and public address (PA) system is in one room and the dining area is in another, it can be difficult for the announcements made by the entertainer to be heard by all the guests, and coordinating the reception events can be tricky. If the venue has multiple floors, it becomes even more of a nightmare.

Regardless of how attractive using that beautiful old mansion or clubhouse might be, a venue that is located all in one room, such as a ballroom, is recommended. Again, multiple rooms become difficult to manage for any Master of Ceremonies, and many will miss important parts of the program because of the separation. Although a venue that has multiple floors may have the acoustical systems necessary for communicating throughout the site, it may still be difficult for some guests to move through different rooms to participate in socializing, dancing, or specialty activities like the bouquet and garter tosses.

Tents

Tents are almost a necessity for outdoor events. Both indoor and outdoor events may use tents to expand the environment. A tent may add or detract from the ambiance depending upon its quality and functionality. If inclement weather is a factor, a sturdy, professional tent can save the event. Tents can serve as much more than just a shell. Many have inner linings, walls, lights, heating, and even floors—including dance floors. Some wealthy people at very high-end events use tents. Chelsea Clinton's wedding took place in a tent that cost $600,000!

Bear in mind that using a tent as an overflow room creates problems, as previously mentioned in the discussion regarding venues with multiple rooms.

#20 I didn't know half of the "other things" required for a tent.

When using a tent, there are additional things to consider, including lights and power, which are necessary for the entertainment. Most tents use chain lighting, where one light is daisy chained to the next. This puts a lot of power consumption on one outlet. In many cases, a simple extension cord is used to supply power to a tent. This is inadequate, if you are going to have any form of entertainment requiring more power.

Adequate power is the most common issue. As mentioned, so many items require power—general lighting, hotplates, coffeemakers, heat lamps, fans, heaters, videographer and photographer lighting, as well as the entertainment equipment. The DJ alone can cause a breaker to blow by using equipment that draws a large amount of power. Some lighting, amps, fans, fog machines, etc., take an enormous amount of power.

Although rare, generators are sometimes used. They too have issues in handling the power load. Bear in mind that some generators can be noisy. On that note, it is advisable to use multiple lines from multiple locations with current ratings necessary to prevent a power failure.

#21 We lost all power at our event.

As you can imagine, having the circuit breaker pop during the event can put a damper on a reception. Outdoor tents use a tremendous amount of power for lighting, as well as for the entertainment, not to mention that required for heaters and environment makers (fog machines, specialty lighting, etc.). Having separate power lines dedicated for separate uses will ensure a greater likelihood of success. Another concern is that water with power in a tent during a storm could be dangerous.

Ensure that all outlets are above ground level. Most professional tent companies that provide power will tie-wrap the ends of cords six to ten inches up a pole for safety. It is never wise to remain in a tent during a violent storm. Seek safer shelter, and return after the storm has passed.

#22 It's too hot; it's too cold.

Unless your tent is equipped with the right equipment to make your guests comfortable, the weather would have to be on your side to maintain moderate temperatures. Guests will be constantly going in and out of the tent. If the tent is enclosed with walls and doors, those seated just inside the tent doors could become uncomfortable. Gas heaters are great to heat tents, but guests seated in front of the heaters are usually subjected to massive heat. Another concern is gas fumes from portable heaters. Be sure there's proper ventilation, so your guests are comfortable and safe.

Wind can also be a major factor. Under the best circumstances, the tent flaps can be raised and a wonderful breeze enjoyed. But a torrential storm can displace all the beautiful decorations throughout the tent. In other words, without optimal conditions or prior planning, tents can cause multiple problems.

Plainly speaking, tents are a gamble. Yes, they usually look beautiful in the movies, and everyone appears to be having a great time, but there is nothing like being indoors for having all the conveniences close at hand.

#23 It was no fun getting our feet wet.

Tents do not have floors, unless they're set up over decking or a cemented area, or you pay to have a dance floor laid (which is very expensive). Tents are typically raised on the grass . . . not great for expensive shoes (or inexpensive shoes for that matter). A few preventive measures can avoid those circumstances. Place the tent in an area with good drainage and adequate power, and be sure the grass is cut low. Have an alternative plan in case the weather is so bad you simply must relocate (or reschedule). An event I was hired for was to be held in a tent on the waterfront but had to be postponed because of Hurricane Irene. Fortunately, the new date turned out to be a beautiful evening.

Even if the tent is set up on concrete, rain can still cause problems. At one reception, inclement weather caused water about two inches deep to flow across the floor of the tent. All the entertainment equipment had to be set up on the dance floor, which happened to be three inches high and the only dry spot under the tent.

#24 We really got "bugged."

Insects can also be a major nuisance. Depending on the time of year, time of day, and location, bugs can ruin your outdoor event.

A tourist city with beautiful beaches tempts many brides to consider the oceanfront as the ideal location for their ceremony. Unfortunately, the seashore has its share of disadvantages. One Saturday in July, the sand was so hot that most of the guests opted to keep their shoes on. The bride planned well and had coolers filled with water and a basket of fans on hand. But the ladies ended up using the fans to shoo sand flies away from their ankles. Insect repellant would have been more effective, but, in a pinch, the fans worked fairly well.

Be prepared by spraying beforehand. Having citronella candles or torches on hand is also a good idea and can even add a touch of romantic ambiance.

#25 We don't have a dance floor.

Most dance floors are made of wood and, in most circumstances, rental companies will not allow their dance floors to be ruined because of a wet environment. Some rental companies have plastic, rubber, and even metal floors. Regardless, they will still not jeopardize an expensive dance floor if mud and moisture can damage it. Make sure the location of the tent is suitable for the rental company—or your guests will end up dancing on the grass.

Do They Really Need to Eat?

The Care and Feeding of Your Guests

#26 My vendors are not the professionals I thought they were.

It's not unusual to make multiple major purchases in your lifetime, like automobiles, houses, even businesses. It is, however, unusual to shop more than once for a wedding reception. Even though, sadly, in today's society many may have multiple marriages, most people still don't have more than one extravagant reception.

I encountered such a situation when a bride entered my office for a consultation. When I recognized her, I gently asked what had happened. She began by telling me how much she had enjoyed her first reception and then explained the cause of the demise of her marriage. Despite the sad circumstances, I was delighted that she was pleased with my services and wanted to hire me again.

Get references. The only way to know if a vendor is going to be a true professional at your event is to find out how the vendor performed at previous events. There are always exceptions. If a vendor works closely with a venue or another vendor, don't be surprised if one will refer the other even if one or both are not highly rated. Even though referral fees are technically illegal in most places, they are commonplace among vendors in the industry. An example would be a venue that refers one particular entertainer only. Either there is some form of nepotism, a kickback, or the entertainer is the best in town. Do the research on your own. Ask for references, and check into the level of professionalism they portray.

#27 I contracted one vendor but got a different one.

Unfortunately, that's not as unusual as you'd think. Meet the vendors in person. Make an appointment and invest a little time with the vendors you are contracting. Do not be satisfied with a casual conversation over the phone and a faxed or mailed contract. Imagine ordering red flowers and ending up with pink flowers at your event. Some DJ companies are notorious for promising a popular personality or entertainer, and delivering an inexperienced teenager with a home stereo. Ask, *"Are you going to be the DJ who performs at my reception? If not, who is?"* Inquire about reputations. Everyone has one! If they don't, then you can expect an inexperienced vendor. One of the best referrals for any vendor is word of mouth. Ask your friends and/or family. If you attend an event before planning your own, pay attention to the details. Don't be afraid to ask for a business card if you find the vendor to be professional.

#28 I chose the wrong caterer.

Many venues have their own catering staffs and

prohibit outsourcing of other services. Because of this, brides and the grooms must look beyond the beautiful ballroom, the luxurious foyer, and the extravagant gardens. Ask for a taste. Talk about your choices and think about what your guests would enjoy. Let's face it, food is important. Without it, people get grumpy and downright disgruntled. Your guests may be disappointed if you serve hotdogs and beans. Not that you can't serve those—it all depends on what kind of reception you plan to have (we'll talk more about that in another chapter).

The caterer you choose can have a lot to do with the location of your function. Some specialty caterers will prepare a feast of courses (for a price, of course). Others will delight your guests with barbecue to die for. Then there are the "bulk market" frozen food preparers. If food is high on your list of priorities, you should pay close attention to the venue and your ability to change caterers to one who can better meet your needs.

#29 I selected the wrong food.

Just because a venue can provide food doesn't mean the product is worthy of your special day. Don't assume that because the venue is nice that their food service is comparable. Doing your homework and research is essential. Many establishments provide food tastings or provide a list of references. A recent client conveyed how disappointed she was in the food at her reception, saying the bread was like a rock, the meat like shoe leather, and the dessert still frozen when served.

What kind of food should you feed your guests? The answer lies in your guests and how much money you have available to please them. Notice that I mentioned pleasing *your guests* and not you. Your goal should be to have your guests raving about your event.

#30 I blew my entire budget on the meal.

There's a wide span of tastes and a wide range of prices to meet those tastes. So much emphasis is placed on impressing our friends, rather than pleasing the bride and groom while not going into debt. An extravagant meal is nice, but the question is, is it necessary or is "ordinary" good enough? There is no doubt that in a crowd of a hundred people, there are always a few food critics. Most won't care if the meal is pizza or beef; they'll place the emphasis on whether they're having a good time. A professional caterer or hotel kitchen can provide hors d'oeuvres of cheese and fruit or artichoke hearts and caviar. The meal can span from ham sandwiches to seafood and steak. You truly need to judge if the meal is going to be the focal point of the day.

#31 I spent too much./I should have spent more.

Let's look at the bottom of the scale in terms of cost. When I say low in cost, I don't mean low in taste or quality. In many cases, having family and friends cook the food to feed your guests is as good as it gets, but there are some drawbacks. If you're having a potluck or backyard picnic, having family and friends work on a day that should be enjoyed by all can keep them from enjoying the wedding. They can miss out on important parts of the event and be hard to locate for important photos.

Having professionals prepare meals even for a less-than-formal event will provide an environment where everyone can have fun. Serving hamburgers and hot dogs can do the trick if your wedding reception is catered around a backyard picnic environment. The other end of the spectrum, involving chefs and meals that are flown in from other countries, don't always go as well as one would expect.

#32 I didn't order enough food.

Another factor is quantity versus quality. Most venues plan with you to make sure that adequate food is prepared for your guests. Part of the secret is to be "careful what you ask for." "Inviting guests" is a subject for another section, but be careful how many guests you invite. Statistically speaking, if you invite 100 guests, 80 to 90 will RSVP that they will attend. Of those 80 to 90, only 75 will actually show. If you order food for 100, be prepared to have some extra food. If your invitation is less formal in nature and your invitation includes "and guest" or "the more the merrier," again, be careful. There have been occasions when more guests arrive than were expected. At one such event, only 150 people were expected, but closer to 250 attended. This placed the chef and his staff in a dilemma. This was not the first time the fridge was raided to feed the extra guests. Yes, even hotdogs. This didn't reflect well on those who had promised to serve a nice meal to guests. Make sure you ask your caterer beforehand: Can you make more food if needed?

#33 The meal was served at the wrong time.

So far, the day is going along pretty well, and you're happy with how everything is turning out. The ceremony was only 15 to 20 minutes longer than estimated. Not unusual. (The bride's delay in getting to the church on time was good exercise for the groom's heart.) The photographer takes over to make sure memories are captured, and a few extra pictures are taken. There goes another 15 to 20 minutes. Your wedding party is finally in the limousine en route to the venue. Then one of the groomsman yells out, "Stop at the 7-11! I need a pack of cigarettes!" The limo driver pulls over, and two or three jump out because they needed to use the restroom. (No need to tell you why.) There goes another 10 minutes. You finally arrive at the reception, where your guests have been waiting patiently (hopefully).

The food, however, was prepared and ready to be served nearly an hour ago. A few guests have most likely complained (to themselves and to each other), and your mother is probably angry with the caterer.

Most venues will coordinate with you on the timing. Most of the time, this is good in that there are no worries associated with when the meal will be served. As you can imagine, having the meal scheduled too early can cause conflicts. Having too long between your arrival at the venue and the beginning of the meal can cause an awkward lull. The food can overcook or dry out. Coordinate with your venue, caterer, and entertainment for the best timing. You must also coordinate with the professionals at the ceremony—from the officiate (or individual performing the ceremony) to the photographer to the limo driver (or whoever is bringing you from the ceremony to the reception).

#34 I chose the wrong way to serve the meal.

Keep in mind the time it takes to serve and eat the meal. Depending on the size of your group and the timeline of your event, having your guests serve themselves at a buffet is typically the most expedient. Due to the time it takes to have a large group served, a plated and served meal may cause serious conflicts with your entire event. While a plated meal is usually cheaper, it may take twice as long to serve and eat. If you have invited more than 150 people, expect a plated meal to take nearly two hours. That may cause conflicts with timelines in your entertainment, and some of your guests may be annoyed with the delay in being fed. A buffet seems less formal, but guests typically prefer being fed quickly and choosing for themselves the amount and types of food they prefer.

Although being fed a plated meal seems more luxurious, it is often cheaper. But if you're expecting a large group, be aware that one end of the room will be finishing their meal while the other end may just have been served. You will have to allow perhaps an extra hour for plated meals, which will decrease the amount of dancing and fun activities you may desire.

It's true—it's all about the meal at some venues and situations. There's nothing wrong with having a four, five, or even an eight-course meal. Simply expect less time on the dance floor. In some cultures, it's not unusual to have one course, then have an activity (such as dancing), then the next course, another activity, and so on.

#35 I put my family and friends to work.

Hosting an event is a lot of work. If you are going to feed a hundred people, one or two individuals would be overwhelmed by the amount of work it takes to prepare meals for large numbers. The savings would be the biggest reason to attempt it. But, in reality, do you want your friends or family members slaving away for hours rather than joining you in having fun at your event? What if something goes wrong? What if the chicken is too spicy or the pasta is overdone? Will you be angry at Aunt Betty? What if the meal is behind schedule? Like two hours behind schedule? What about the mess? Who is going to clean up? There are reasonable caterers that can accommodate various budgets and take care of all the work, so your family and friends can enjoy themselves, and your event can be less stressful.

#36 I don't want my mother working on my special day.

Do you really want your mom working on your wedding day? Your budget will determine many aspects of your day, including whether or not you will hire professionals to prepare your food (versus amateurs). While there is nothing wrong with having your mother and her friends prepare the feast for your guests, seriously consider if you really want to subject them all to working rather than enjoying the day. With a local caterer, the job can be accomplished within your budget, and your family and guests can enjoy themselves without doing all the work.

The part-time fish fry, pig-pickin' barbecue, weekend warriors can satisfy any number of guests and are generally reasonably priced. People also feel a bit more relaxed at a less-than-formal event. Keep in mind that your food choice will have a direct impact on your guests' impressions. It's often true that six months after the wedding, guests will not remember whether they were served chicken or steak, but they'll remember if they had a good (or bad) time.

Working our way up a notch, some mobile caterers can arrive in a fleet of trucks and specialty trailers to perform a well-orchestrated food fest. In many cases, these mobile food kitchens are a good answer to small venue needs or backyard functions. Many of these catering services will also include the china, silverware, and linens. It's important that these services work closely with the other professionals involved in your event, including florist, cake baker, and entertainer. For example, the entertainer may announce when the food is ready and call the tables to the buffet. A close relationship should also exist for purposes of coordinating the special dances, toasts, etc.

Many locations offer extensive kitchens that can be used by catering services. Most caterers prepare the food at an alternate site and transport the food by truck using hot boxes. The local kitchen at the venue gives the catering staff the opportunity to re-warm food and prepare the lighter hors d'oeuvres and cold foods.

#37 The catering staff didn't work well with the other professionals.

Although your catering staff and entertainment are typically under two different umbrellas, they must work closely together to coordinate the event. The food service staff must work in harmony with the entertainer, as he (or she) is often directly responsible for making sure the event runs smoothly. The question that isn't asked enough is: *Will you work with the entertainment?* Everything from the introduction of wedding party, to the announcement of the hors d'oeuvres and the bar being open, the calling of tables to visit the buffet, the coordination of the pouring of the champagne for the toasts and the cake cutting, the tossing of the bouquet and the garter—all must be coordinated through the entertainer.

The catering staff's responsibility includes pouring the champagne for a champagne toast. Some entertainers plan every moment of an event to the point where it is choreographed like a stage play. Some venues prefer to have the toast performed earlier due to the expense of keeping a catering staff on premises for that very purpose. Without the coordination between the catering staff and the entertainment, expect the catering staff to simply pour champagne then tug on the entertainer's shirtsleeve, reporting that the champagne has been poured even though it isn't yet time for the toast. There's nothing like having warm champagne for a toast (or having the guests drink it before the toast), or cutting a portion of the activities to redirect the toast earlier because of an uncaring or irresponsible catering staff.

#38 The wedding cake was too small/too big.

The wedding cake is more than just a dessert. The bride and groom "serve" the cake to each other, symbolizing that they will serve each other for the rest of their lives. Having enough cake for each guest permits everyone to partake in the tradition.

Traditionally, the top layer of the cake is preserved for the bride and groom to celebrate their first anniversary. Many couples today aren't concerned with tradition, and many forget to take the cake top with them. The catering staff has been known to chase after the departing couple with the top layer in a box. Or they try to locate the couple after the reception.

The catering staff has also mistakenly cut the top tier and served it to guests when the cake has been too small. On the other hand, there have been cakes so large that the mother of the bride has begged guests to take extra slices home with them, reminding single girls of the tradition that sleeping with a wedding cake under their pillows is said to bring dreams of their true loves.

The catering staffs and bakers, if worth their salt, know the correct size your cake should be based on the number of guests expected. Plan well to ensure that not only the style, color, and flavor of your cake is exactly what you want, but that the size is right as well.

#39 "Susie Homemaker" made my cake.

Homemade versus professional . . . that is the question. There is nothing wrong with Aunt Betsy making your wedding cake for you . . . if she has the resources and experience to do it right. I can't tell you how many times brides and family members were in tears because the cake was a depiction of the Leaning Tower of Pisa or had the side smashed during transit. Again, if someone you know has the talent to do it right, then it's perfectly okay. (Note: Be sure "Susie Homemaker" knows how to determine the correct size, or you'll be one of those brides crying, "My wedding cake was too big/small!")

#40 Extravagance ruined my cake.

Have you ever seen a cake with a waterfall in it? Can you imagine someone crying when that waterfall starts leaking? Let me assure you, there's nothing entertaining about it.

Have you ever seen a five-, six-, or even a seven-tiered cake? Have you ever heard the cliché, "The bigger they are, the harder they fall"? It's like building a house of cards. The higher the house, the greater the likelihood of catastrophe. It's true for wedding cakes too. You may want your wedding cake to be the eighth wonder of the world, but extravagance can often cause more problems than oohs and ahs.

Be sensible. Listen to your baker. You can still have a beautiful cake . . . one that will make it to the venue and through the reception without incident.

#41 My cake melted.

Ice cream cakes at weddings? It's (obviously) not a good idea. Also some gelatin-style cakes can melt. Heat is a major concern for some cake makers. Doughnut groom cakes are notorious for melting and making quite a mess. And don't think that winter will naturally alleviate the problem. If it's cold outside, the venue will likely have the heat blasting. You may have issues if your cake is positioned under a heating vent. Research the room ahead of time to find the best spot to place the cake table. A cool, dry place is best.

If you have a summer wedding and plan to hold it outdoors, plan for the heat and the possibility that the cake and the icing can melt. There may also be issues with insects.

Ask your caterer to place a moist towel near the cake table. You may need it after the cake-cutting ceremony and champagne toast.

#42 Kids, fingers, and cakes seem to find each other.

Children don't understand the importance of the wedding cake. They remember seeing a kid brother taking a swipe of the icing while Mom wasn't looking. Just imagine how tempting a large beautiful cake is to a little person. Place the cake in the middle of a larger round table to be out of the reach of munchkins and possible bumps from passersby. Ensure that the table is adequate to hold the weight of the cake.

Plan your cake to your event. Extravagant cakes in less than extravagant places are awkward. Ice cream cakes—on hot or cool days—don't work. While they are a favorite for a "groom's cake," doughnut cakes don't impress.

#43 I am so drunk. The world is beautiful, and everybody loves me.

Nothing, I repeat, *nothing* is as pathetic as a drunken bride or groom. Thousands of dollars are spent on a wedding from the gowns to the venue, and very little of it is remembered the next day when the wedding party imbibes too much alcohol. However, the stories about your behavior will continue for months and, sometimes, years to come.

It often starts off so innocently—just a sip of champagne at the hairdresser's or in the limo, then a glass of courage to calm the nerves, then a few more with dinner. Then the celebration begins and the drinks flow. But afterwards, your mother tells you how embarrassed she was, and all your friends leave early because the scene started looking sloppy and a little ugly.

I'm often asked if not serving alcohol is a major factor for an event. The answer is no. If the environment is welcoming, the entertainment inviting, the food appetizing, and the guests are enjoying themselves, alcohol doesn't even play a role. I have entertained at dozens of events where people have had a great time without intoxicating drinks. I tell my clients that if guests want to drink, they'll find a way. They will either have a drink before they arrive, go to their cars and take a drink, or even bring flasks to take shots in the bathroom. However, you can control what is being served at the event.

#44 A couple of drunks ruined the entire event.

Think about it. There are very few occasions when people have the opportunity to indulge on someone else's dime. Yeah! Open bar! Make that a double!

It is not unusual to see an inconsiderate guest with two drinks in hand, on the dance floor, clutching each glass as if it were his or her best friend.   People all react differently to intoxication. Some are friendly and polite; others mean and rude, while some become sexual deviants or rock stars. It's all part of the fun and games until someone steps out of line and either makes an idiot of him (or her)self or you.

It is distressing to witness a fight at a wedding reception. Once I observed a little ruckus involving individuals from two families. I didn't think much of it at the time, but I was told later that there had been a serious conflict between the families about the alcohol. The bride's family was very conservative and wanted people to have a good time, but not *too* good of a time. The father of the bride did not want to be responsible for anyone getting hurt or jailed the day of his daughter's wedding. He watched the flow of the beer and limited the consumption of those who indulged a bit too much. This ruffled feathers, because the groom's family enjoyed drinking and tended towards risqué behavior. Soon the event had ended and, unlike other events in the groom's family's past, there was alcohol left over. The controversy began when some of the groom's family wanted to take the alcohol with them to an alternate location to continue the party, and the bride's father refused. He said he would not be held responsible for anyone getting hurt or getting into trouble or, worse yet, killing someone because of drunkenness. This started the first family feud. The groom's family finally stormed off to reluctantly purchase their own beer from the local mini-mart.

If it is known that there is an individual or a group of individuals that may in some way jeopardize the event by consuming too much alcohol, then every attempt should be made to avoid the inevitable end . . . perhaps opening the bar a bit later, or closing the bar during dinner, or closing the bar earlier in the evening. You can make the bar a "cash bar" (meaning folks have to pay for their drinks, which is guaranteed to slow the drinking down). Or even have a talk with the person(s) in advance to avoid issues. Having pre-designated duty drivers can help.

#45 I wish I would have planned better when it came to the bar.

Planning thoughtfully can avoid so many problems. Know your guests. Do you want them to get drunk? Sounds silly to ask, but do you? Do you want your elegant wedding reception to be focused around a few people that overindulge? By working with the staff at the venue, the bar can be open during the cocktail hour, then closed during dinner. Opening the bar again after dinner and then finally closing the bar a while before the event ends is often a good idea. At the risk of sounding like a controlling parent, alcohol in moderation is fine at a reception; alcohol in excess is not and can ruin your happy day.

#46 I had to wait for twenty minutes to start our first dance.

I once worked with a bride who was disappointed that she was unable to immediately begin the event with the grand entrance and her first dance because the bar was located next to the dance floor. Some venues don't have extra space when there are a large number of guests. Having the bar adjacent to the dance floor causes problems throughout the evening.

Imagine this: You have ordered your rum and coke and the red wine for your date. You turn to return to your table and get sideswiped by an exuberant dancer. Or there is a less-than-responsible drinker dancing on the dance floor, and he sees no one in line at the bar. He looks at the bartender and orders two more shots. Moments later, the same process occurs again. How long before this doesn't end well?

While working with the event coordinator, talk about the layout of the room. Try to keep the bar away from the dance floor. If the room is still too small, setting up outside the door might work. Either way, having the bar set up right next to the dance floor may become an issue later in the evening.

#47 My mother is still mad at me for my overindulgence.

I've mentioned it a couple times: there is nothing less attractive than seeing a bride or groom intoxicated. There is nothing wrong with having fun. There is nothing wrong with having a couple of drinks—but getting drunk at your wedding is not cool. There's a lot of pressure on brides and grooms. Some find that having a couple of drinks takes the edge off, but—in many cases—alcohol reacts differently the day of a wedding for several reasons. Some brides don't eat right (if at all) and become intoxicated much faster. Wearing a heavy gown and being whisked around from preparation venue to ceremony venue to reception venue can cause a bride to become parched and dehydrated. Drink water! Just like the short story at the beginning of this book, the drinking can start early in the day if permitted. Champagne seems to show up at the hair and makeup setting, then the limo, and even in VIP rooms. Sip, don't gulp!

Of all the events I've performed, only a few ended up with the bride or groom intoxicated. One bride was still attempting to finish a keg with her friends, as I was rolling my equipment out the door. Her husband had already passed out. Not pretty. Another time, a groom downed a bottle of Wild Turkey whiskey before the ceremony. He needed a babysitter the entire evening. Someone had to guide him every step of the way.

Be smart. Decide ahead of time not to overindulge. You'll thank yourself the next morning . . . and every time you look at your wedding photos.

#48 In hindsight, we shouldn't have started doing shots.

You're at the local pub, and karaoke is in the air. Your friends are there, and everyone is having fun. Someone feels generous and orders shots for everyone. Minutes later, someone else orders another round. Soon everyone is laughing and kicking up their heels. Perhaps this memory is what triggers the same behavior to be recreated at your event. Only there are a few differences. The shots at the bar are free for the guests, but dad is paying the bill. And because of so many factors mentioned already, the outcome is not the same. Be responsible. Tell the bar not to serve "shots." If you choose to indulge, do so in moderation.

The bride and groom's overindulgence and the guests are two distinct issues. Alcohol is at times detrimental, and the point is always to limit the quantity and hope for the best. I tell my brides to never "tie-one-on" the day of the celebration. One can never completely control the guests.

Entertaining the Troops

What Will They Remember?

#49 The band is too loud.

There are pros and cons to having a band versus having a disc jockey. In most situations, bands are too loud for a close environment. It is nearly impossible for a band to play at a tone suitable for cocktail and dinner hours.

#50 Who is acting as Master of Ceremonies?

Bands are talented at playing certain types of music. Seldom are they capable of acting as masters of ceremonies. Performing such duties takes skills in addition to being simply a musician or singer.

#51 The band is on break, and it's eerily quiet in the room.

It's called dead air. Again, bands have drawbacks. Breaks are one of them. Some bands are professional and take short breaks, while others have no idea of the importance of their performance to the overall success of the event. In the DJ world, dead air is considered unprofessional and is frowned upon.

#52 The band can't play my request.

It's a common complaint. Compared to a DJ, bands have limited repertoires and usually have a set list of songs. Bands are usually more expensive and don't have the flexibility of a disc jockey. Having a band *and* a DJ working as Master of Ceremony (emcee) can offer the benefits of both worlds.

#53 The DJ mispronounced half the names during our grand entrance.

Let's face it, we are a nation of many different ethnic backgrounds and family heritages. Some names are difficult to pronounce, but this is no excuse for the individual who is announcing the Grand Entrance. Meeting with your entertainer, whether it be the band, a DJ, or even a wedding singer, should ensure that the names of the wedding party and the groomsmen are pronounced correctly. This requires planning and professionalism on the part of the entertainer. If a name is particularly difficult to pronounce, consider writing the name out phonetically so the entertainer doesn't have to rely on memory to pronounce the name correctly.

#54 Our DJ had some fantastic equipment, but he was still disappointing.

Having the best equipment is fine, but not knowing what to do with it can still blow a party. While an iPod is a great device for some purposes, it doesn't replace a DJ at a ceremony or reception. An entertainer needs to be a personality, a roadie, and a wedding coordinator. In other words, it takes more than just good equipment. One needs talent and even the ability to speak clearly and succinctly. A high school kid may be the next superstar, but his/her home stereo equipment is probably inferior and not suitable for importable occasions. It takes a combination of professional equipment, skill, and experience.

#55 The DJ played exactly what I asked him to play, but it didn't turn out as I expected.

Any DJ that permits the client to choose all the music is setting him/herself and the event up for failure. A young bride once insisted that I play only from a limited stack of CDs that most people had never heard. I made the mistake of agreeing. Only 45 minutes into the cocktail hour her dad approached me and said, "What in the world are you playing?" I gently told him that these were the "must plays" that his daughter insisted on. He said, "I'll take care of this," and walked away. A few minutes later, the bride approached me and said, "You were right. Play what you think is best." I changed the music and, before long, a guest said, "Thank you for changing the music. I was about to go nuts!"

Give your entertainer the flexibility when it comes to requests. If he is a professional, you can trust him to know which requests will add to or detract from the ambiance of your event.

#56 The DJ didn't show up. / Our DJ was late.

It's not unheard of. Just like any other business, there are different levels of professionalism. Some DJs may go out of business before the event date and not notify their clients. Some take a higher paying gig. Some simply forget. Some DJs work alone as single entity companies and not as a team with multiple DJs. Single-entity companies run the greatest risk of such things happening. In today's world, the Internet is another factor. An unwitting bride shopping for a DJ can come across a website claiming to provide a professional disc jockey at a reasonable rate. These companies typically charge less than local companies and simply act as booking agents. It is not unusual for these companies to call a local DJ service to subcontract an event. As these companies work on the concept of quantity and not quality, in most cases they have never met the DJ, nor have they verified references or experience. Once they have received the deposit and have made the pass to the "cheap" DJ, there is rarely any follow up ensuring the DJ is on track to perform the event. Hiring a DJ through a reputable, professional company with multiple DJs is the best option.

As an entertainer, nothing is more unprofessional than to be setting up your equipment as the guests are walking in the door. A professional will allow adequate time to arrive, set up, perform sound checks, and even change clothes before the guests arrive. Again, it is a sure sign of an amateur to be unprepared when the guests arrive. Those who don't plan accordingly (or who are working by the hour and don't want to invest any more time than absolutely necessarily) eventually end up running late. But the professional shows up early, having anticipated and planned for unexpected, unforeseen events. Those who are less than professional will wait till the last minute to load equipment, depart, and setup. Vehicle issues, personal issues, or equipment issues all cause them to be late and not only shed a bad light on them as pros, but detract from the event overall.

#57 The DJ doesn't seem to be playing the right music.

The DJ may not *have* the "right" music. As you know, music is expensive. You can't expect a young or inexperienced DJ to have a large musical repertoire, nor can you expect him to know all the musical genres required for satisfying all clients. This takes years of investment and experience. Meet with the DJ early in your planning to ensure that he/she has the "right" kind of music for your event.

#58 The music doesn't sound right.

Have you ever attended an event where the sound coming out of the speakers was nearly painful? The entire sequence of music and sound is only as good as the "weakest link in a chain." Scratches or smudges on a CD can cause problems and can disrupt a smooth flow of music. Some DJs download music from the Internet. This medium is less than desirable for professional sound systems, because it amplifies the imperfections. The level of the professional sound system is also a factor. Everything from the CD player to the amplifier can cause distortion in playback. The most significant of all hardware problems are the speakers. The speakers should be professional and mounted on stands to emit sound correctly. Hiring a professional company should ensure the best sound for your event.

#59 My guests and I couldn't understand anything that was said, and the music was muffled.

The acoustics at any venue are of paramount importance. Some sites have vaulted ceilings that pose a challenge for any entertainer. Other venues require extra or modified equipment to achieve a suitable level of performance value. Some locations have hard, flat walls that reflect sound too much causing echoes and feedback. The best acoustic venues have some variety in the walls, along with decorations or variances in the materials to absorb sounds. Drapes, trees, and even people help make sounds and vocal acoustics more pleasurable.

One of the best ways to avoid problems is to hire a professional. Discuss the acoustically challenges of a room beforehand to be sure your entertainer has the equipment and the know-how to solve any sound issues. I have had to place third wireless center punch speakers in other parts of the room to fill the vocal frequencies. In layman's terms, a third speaker in another part of the room can assist in keeping a room from being an echo chamber. Another method used by some professionals is to crossfire the speakers. In other words, the two main speakers on each side of the room can be pointed to a cross-point in the middle of the room to keep the sound from bouncing back off a flat wall.

#60 Everyone had a great time, except Grandma who complained about how loud the music was.

While the consensus is that most elderly folks don't like loud music, my research shows this to be only partially true. Complaints about how loud music is may not really be the issue; the problem may be the type of music being played. For instance, if you play hip-hop to a group of seniors, any level will be uncomfortable for most; they simply don't like the style. And vice versa, try playing oldies to a younger crowd, and you'll have the same problem. In most cases, the bride and groom or the event coordinator seats the VIPs (bridal party, family members) closest to the dance floor as a sign of preference and honor. Seating older folks farther away from the speakers and the dance floor typically makes them more comfortable. It's easier for them to converse with others, and they will usually not complain about the music being too loud. Those who have tried my suggestion have thanked me for being so thoughtful.

Certain decibels do become uncomfortable for certain age groups, especially if they wear hearing aids. But a professional DJ should have performed sound checks before the event and will know the proper levels for the room size and number of people in the room.

#61 My guests were offended by the music the DJ played.

One of the drawbacks of using younger, less experienced and less professional DJs is that they are often unable to invest in professional, subscribed "radio-edit" material. Even those who own radio-edited material should not play lyrically-challenged songs that can offend guests at your reception.

#62 The DJ offended my guests with inappropriate comments.

An innocent slip of the tongue can happen to anyone, but a true professional would know better than to make any comments over the microphone that could in any way offend your guests. A professional DJ knows when to "shut up" and let the music do the talking. Making clear, concise announcements and taking care of all the necessary microphone work in a pleasant, professional manner sets the tone for a successful event.

#63 The DJ doesn't/can't make announcements.

Some DJs are minimalists. They attempt to go through any and every event by playing music and refraining from the interaction necessary for special events, such as receptions.

Some DJs are very good at playing music. Some emcees are great at running a show and making all the announcements necessary to keep an event on track. But some emcees can't play music—and, worse yet, some DJs don't have a clue how to be an emcee.

The problem, at times, stems from the expectations of the clients. For an example, a DJ may know exactly what songs to play for a group of people, like club clientele. But when it comes time to say a few words, nothing but a canned suggestion like, "Don't forget to tip your bartenders and waitresses," is all he can muster. Anything beyond that is not on his resume. Not all DJs are public speakers. Being an emcee is a skill—a talent. Surveys reveal that one of people's greatest fears is speaking in public.

Jerry Seinfeld jokes, *"According to most studies, people's number one fear is public speaking. Number two is death. Death is number two. Does that seem right? That means to the average person, if you have to go to a funeral, you're better off in the casket than doing the eulogy."* Of course that's a joke. If confronted with the choice of dying or speaking in public, no one would choose dying. But the fact remains that it takes talent, skill, and experience to speak well in front of a group—especially with a microphone in your hand.

Having someone perform a "Grand Entrance" for what is one of the most important days in a couple's life—

and then destroying it in a half a dozen ways because of lack of experience or a simple lack of command of the English language is sad in many respects. For that very reason, some DJs/emcees will avoid making any announcements beyond the very minimum. This alone can tarnish what may have been a fabulous event.

Ask if the entertainer, whether a band or a DJ, will be making all the general announcements. Ask if there will be any further use of the microphone for interaction or motivation (like encouragement to dance). Ask (or do the research) if the entertainer has the experience to put on a show, or if he's only capable of playing music. A band may call that individual a "wedding singer." DJs use the title of *emcee*.

#64 My Maid of Honor was in charge of the music.

At any given event, a wide variety of musical tastes will set the tone for your entire day. Depending on the age of the bride and groom, the guests can include everyone from your great-grandfather to baby Louie. For your reception to be a success, the right music must be played to satisfy all musical tastes. Try to imagine how many songs existed in the 20s or 30s. As you might guess, there are a lot more now and more coming out every day.

What this means for your entertainer is that it should be rather easy for him or her to satisfy the individuals desiring "older" music. Back in the day, there were just a handful of artists and musical styles. Taking a request from an elderly fellow so he may relive the romance of so many years ago and being able to play that request can set the tone for the entire wedding party. My point is that a wide variety of music is almost a necessity to establish a loving atmosphere.

65

A happy medium must be reached to satisfy everyone. While a loud band may be overkill, having no music at all would result in an eerily quiet atmosphere. The Maid of Honor may like punk rock or rap and insist that the DJ play her favorite style of music. This may not go over well if the bride and groom like country or rock. Regardless, having the responsibility to be in charge of the music requires more than setting up an iPod and pressing play. Research must be done, including whether the entertainer has the ability to provide a wide variety of music. A professional DJ will take several things into consideration when playing for a diverse group like wedding guests.

Is the average age group is closer to that of Mom and Dad or of a college frat party? Would the group prefer Hip-Hop or a country two-step? What "must plays" did the bride and groom request? Are there any musical genres that have been banned? Again, it all boils down to having a wide variety of genres and having the professional ability to segue through them throughout the event.

#65 My venue is only allowing the DJ an hour to set up.

Many factors influence the time needed to prepare. In most cases, one to two hours are all that are needed for a professional to set up and check the equipment. It's a good idea to check with the venue to see if an event is planned before yours. If there is, this can cause a conflict with both the caterer and your DJ. On the other hand, you wouldn't want your entertainer to show up a half hour to moments prior to your event. This causes undue stress on everyone. Any entertainer that comes late shows an unwelcome lack of professionalism. More often than not, a professional will show up early and do all the sight and sound checks well before the first guests arrive. This has another advantage. If your timeline is off and everything seems to be early, it would be nice to have the music starting exactly when your guests arrive.

It would be a mistake to assume the person you choose will be ready well in advance. Make sure to ask, "What time will you be setting up?"

#66 We have music but no lights.

It's interesting to note that lights are used by bands and DJs. The difference is that bands direct the lights towards themselves, thereby becoming the focal point, while DJs use their lights to entertain the guests. Light shows are not necessary, but they are certainly a fun tool to help establish a more enjoyable environment. Ask your entertainer if a light show is part of the package provided.

#67 I can't believe the fire alarm went off.

Fog can be used by your entertainer to create a unique, romantic environment. Most fog machines are water based and will not bother your guests nor affect those with sensitive eyes.

The key here is the difference between two words—fog and smoke. Research has been done on the psychological effect of fog on people. It is not unusual to see people fanning their faces or making coughing gestures when entering a cloud of fog. Some may even complain that it is affecting their asthma. When told that it is simply compressed moisture and that it will actually moisten their eyes and help them breathe easier because it acts like a humidifier, they suddenly change their reactions.

Older smoke machines that use oil can cause problems for people with breathing issues. These older machines can activate some fire alarms. Most of the newer machines are odorless, but solutions can be added for aromatic atmospheres.

Fog machines are also available in a variety of styles that simply create a mist that fills the entire room. This effect intensifies powerful lights that might be on display. Crawling fog is created by using dry ice. This effect is interesting but a little spooky. It can be used to create the effect of the bride and groom walking out on a magic carpet. Finally, a haze machine provides a similar effect but in a finer mist that tends to last a bit longer. The latter machines are more expensive and may not be available through your average DJs. Regardless, always be sure to check with the venue before using fog.

#68 Grandma is in the hospital with a broken hip.

Bubbles spilled on the floor or a bubble machine causing a slick could result in a bride spending her honeymoon in a hip cast—or her grandmother ending up in the hospital.

The once-traditional rice and birdseed are no longer permitted at most churches and venues, and it seems that bubbles have taken their place. If used properly, bubbles can be romantic and interactive. Photographers love interactive features with bubbles, because they add another dimension to pictures. Professionals can use bubbles to their advantage and make a memorable moment for any couple.

Bubble machines, however, can be problematic and potentially hazardous. They create puddles of slippery soap directly in front of the machine. It's recommended that if bubbles are desired, use the small personal bottles and let your guests set the scene.

#69 My wedding turned into a karaoke-bar night.

If you enjoy hanging out with your friends at the local pub drinking a few "adult" beverages and singing your favorite classics, you might think that would be fun at your wedding reception. Maybe. But it most likely wouldn't be. Remember where the focus should be: on the bride and groom. Whoever is holding the microphone becomes the center of attention—all the focus is transferred to him/her. That's fine if your dad or your pastor is saying the blessing or the best man is giving the toast. But if Uncle Bob has had a few drinks and thinks he's Frank Sinatra (or, worse yet, Bon Jovi), then you have a situation on your hands. Having multiple guests taking turns at the microphone singing bores those not interested. The key to a successful event is to keep as many people interested in all activities as long as possible.

A good compromise is ensuring the singers are good and having the songs sung to the bride and groom. Review the songs in advance and be sure they are appropriate for the event. Lastly, have the entertainer invite the guests to dance while the singer is performing. An exception would be if someone is singing for the bride and groom's first dance, the father/daughter dance, or another special dance.

People Management Skills

Making It Through the Day— from Parents to Rug Rats

#70 I have two dads. How should I handle the father/daughter dance?

It is not uncommon to have multiple sets of parents at a wedding reception. Today, divorced parents are the norm, not the exception. Couples only have their original parents about 25 percent of the time. As a result, brides and grooms have concerns about the politically correct thing to do in order not to cause riffs.

I first ask if there is animosity among the divorced parents. If there is, I suggest that the bride and groom talk with all parties and ask them to put their differences aside for just one day. Perhaps it will be the beginning of a cordial relationship for future events in the bride and groom's life (such as the birth of grandchildren and other special events and holidays).

I'm often asked if there should be two dances—one for the father and one for the stepfather. I believe that the best and most appropriate way to keep things equal and fair is to begin with one dad, then have the second dad cordially "tap out" (not knock out!) the first, and finish the dance with the bride.

#71 It's my wedding, but my mom thinks it's her party.

Controlling mothers, sometimes called "momzillas," may expect to have way too much input into the planning and logistics of wedding receptions. Some forget the event is to celebrate that the bride and groom just got married. Some parents are so controlling that they want to choose everything from the overall theme to the music. Again, while input and parental guidance is good, being a micromanager and taking over a wedding reception as if it were their own party is over the top. Grandparents can also cause similar issues.

Many variables are involved here. A traditional "American" wedding is all about the bride. Parents at times want so much to be a driving force to make their daughter's wedding reception perfect that they forget to involve the bride in some of the decisions made. Often a mother's and daughter's tastes can be complete opposites, and forcing certain things on the bride simply causes arguments.

Going back to variables, there are many different traditions throughout the endless corners of the planet. For example, I once emceed an event for an African couple. Mom was introduced with her friends and Dad was introduced with his entire entourage. The bride and groom entered the room, sat in a pre-positioned area on what looked like a pair of thrones, and were required to be silent and observe the event without interaction. In other words, the wedding reception was all about the parents. The celebration was all about having the father having cast out his daughter to another man and another family. There was no first dance, no bouquet or garter toss, no cake-cutting ceremony. Dad was as proud as a peacock and was serenaded by his entourage all evening.

My point is that everyone is different, and having a clear idea of what's going to happen in advance is a better way of ensuring a successful event.

#72 My parents totally embarrassed me, shedding a bad light on my reception.

When planning your ceremony and reception, you hope your parents will be supportive, loving, and generous. Unfortunately, some turn out to be totally self-involved. At the reception, alcohol sometimes plays a role in parents speaking their minds about the other family or even the bride and/or groom. Some are divorced and, still harboring animosity, may use an event like a wedding reception to vent. A death in the family may also cause some parents to show too much emotion, thereby causing discomfort for the hosts. Some simply have anger issues.

Plan well to avoid any chance of issues arising unexpectedly. I personally coach all my brides and grooms to avoid ever having parents making any announcements on the microphone. There are some exceptions, like when parents choose to welcome the guests or when they act as Matron of Honor or Best Man and give a toast. By tradition, moms or dads should give a toast at the rehearsal dinner, where the environment is easier to control. (More on toasts later.)

#73 I can't believe my parents invited all *their* friends.

If you are wondering why half the guests are leaving early, it could be that their bedtimes are quickly approaching (if not already passed). The people invited to your reception will have *everything* to do with the outcome of the event. A wedding is often considered to be a combination of several things: a family reunion, a belated birthday party, an excuse for Mom and Dad to show off by inviting their friends, a nightclub experience, a kid's romper room, and even church. Your guests should be a mixture of family and friends. Mom may think that, since she's footing the bill, she can invite her bridge club members and dad can bring his golf buddies.

A less-than-fun event might be expected when dozens of mature friends of your parents have been invited and only a limited number of your friends will be there. However, I have witnessed many events where the older guests were having the most fun and actually set the upbeat tone for the event.

These are all things that should be taken into consideration when making the invitation list. Talk to your parents if they are planning to invite friends, and ensure that their guests will be an asset.

People should not be invited just to fill seats—especially at the high prices of today's caterers. Some older, more mature folks will accept your invitation for a free meal and excitement beyond the television much sooner than the younger set that doesn't know what's on their schedule next week (never mind four to five months from now). On that note, if you want a good mixture, invite twice as many young people as those who are not so young. If you want to create a nightclub scene, then invite mostly young people. If you want to go to bed early . . . well, you get the idea.

#74 I only invited 150 guests, but there must be 300 people here. (Or—only half the guests who said they'd come actually showed.)

I've seen it happen. The wedding reception was planned for 150 guests, but 300 people came. How could that happen, you ask? As the entertainer, I started to worry since I brought equipment for an event for no more than 200 people. Every chair at every table was occupied, yet more and more people were arriving. Soon there was standing room only, and all the food at the hors d'oeuvres table was gone. The caterer asked what was going on, as only enough food had been prepared for 150 people. They were asked to do whatever they could to accommodate the guests. Believe it or not, hotdogs began to appear.

It took a little investigative work, but it was soon discovered that a few key people were told when they were invited that it was okay if they wanted to invite a couple of other people—almost as if it were a block party. A few extra invitations and—presto!—the group had doubled. By the way, the dance floor that was large enough for 150 was packed all evening.

Statistics reveal that if you invite 200 people, 175 or so will RSVP. Of those, about 150 will attend. (These figures are not perfect, of course.) To avoid problems, the best you can do is to calculate how many guests you can afford. Send written invitations with specific instructions on whether or not they may bring others, including children. Ask for an RSVP to obtain as accurate a count as possible. Remember, even those who RSVP with a "yes" may not show up—and some who do not respond will attend.

#75 Seventy-five percent of the guests are women. Where are all the men?

While it sounds like a dream for guys, having a lot more women than men at your reception can pose some challenges, especially if your desire is to have a fun party-like atmosphere complete with dancing. It's simply best to have a good, balanced mix of men and women.

When deciding your guest list, aim for an equal number of males and females. If you find that you're inviting a high number of singles, add "and guest" to the invitation to allow for a boyfriend or girlfriend to come along.

#76 My friends left the reception early.

There are many reasons why people leave an event early. A few of these may be:

- Bored/not having fun
- Tasteless food; uninteresting menu
- Less than professional entertainment
- Impolite catering staff
- Temperature uncomfortable (too hot/cold)
- babysitter issues
- Use half of the examples throughout this book

The question one should ask is: how can I plan my reception better? This book will help!

#77 No one wants to dance except the kids.

The main reason adults won't dance is because there

are children running around in circles and spinning donuts on the dance floor. Most adults (and I say most, because some don't care) do not want to take the chance of harming a child by stepping on or knocking him/her over. The adults may have consumed a few drinks by the time the dancing portion of the event rolls around and know that roughhousing kids and tipsy, dancing grownups usually don't mesh.

I call it "kids-on-the-floor syndrome." If there is a dance floor, music, and/or lights, unsupervised children will carouse on the dance floor. The dance floor simply becomes a playground. It's unfortunate that some parents feel no guilt in allowing their kids to run amok, so Mom and Dad can have a good time. Regrettably, kids can practically ruin a wedding reception if they are not kept well in hand. Some adults will leave, while others will simply remain seated and not participate.

What's the best way to avoid this problem? The answer is easy. Don't invite children. What about the flower girl or ring bearer? Having a couple of well-disciplined kids will not be an issue. Some brides and grooms have found alternate ways to solve the kid syndrome. Some hire a young adult to babysit. Some purchase activities and set aside a private table in another area where the children can "hang out." Another idea is to have a special room nearby where they can play with games, movies, or videogames along with a babysitter. Adults can check on them occasionally and still have fun.

#78 Who is watching that child who is terrorizing my event?

We've all seen it. In the store, in the theater, or in the

doctor's office—there's always the unsupervised "mini-terrorist" wreaking havoc. We all ask ourselves, "Who is watching this child?" When this occurs at a wedding or reception, it is most irritating. Do adults truly believe that an event outside of their homes means it's a free-for-all for their kids?

"Let others watch her," they seem to be thinking. Other adults simply prefer to depart early rather than stay and suffer silently. This results in an event imploding.

So that everyone understands, not all children cause problems, nor is it the number of kids (although the fewer the better); it's the behavior of those kids and their parents. In most cases, two or three children fill the roles of ring bearer and flower girl. When there are more children, there are a few things that can be done to offset the typical issues. Hiring a babysitter to be onsite either in the room with the bridal party or in a private room nearby is one solution. This would permit parents to look in on their children and still have a good time. Another idea is to buy some toys from a dollar store and have them in either a nearby room or in special area of the reception.

Thanks for the Memories

Remembering Your Wedding Day

#79 I thought I hired a professional photographer.

Photographers come in all forms from the, "I just got a camera for Christmas, therefore, I must be a photographer" to the "Top Gun" experienced professional. They may be using different formats, but one thing is certain, photographers are only as good as their professional "eye" and their subject.

Some brides want the best photographer and are willing to spend most of their budget on one. She not only wants the professional photographer, she also wants disposable cameras on the tables and a videographer to capture every moment. Then there are others who couldn't care less about formal photos.

As a DJ, I have several pet peeves about photographers. One is equipment. Many photographers arrive at a venue, plop all their bags and equipment in plain sight, not caring one bit about the way it looks or if it makes anyone else look bad. Many photographers believe their job is more important than that of any other professional at the event. That's annoying, primarily because a bit more cooperation with others would probably enable the photographer to take better photos.

Unfortunately, when shopping for a photographer, it isn't possible to determine his or her professional behavior the day of the event. I worked alongside a top-notch photographer who changed the entire environment because of his work habits. The wedding coordinator was asked if a light film of fog could be used during the dancing portion of the program. She came back with a resounding NO. She then mentioned that it was because of the photographer and his desire to take clear pictures. The argument here is: Which is more important at this point, the pictures taken during the dancing portion of the event or the environment created by the entertainer using the tools available? Believe it or not, there was also a complaint made by the photographer that the dance lights ruined a picture because a dot from one of the lights was on the cheek of one of his subjects.

The expense that a bride pays should be calculated based on the value and the product that is expected. The expense is also going to be tied to the experience. When choosing a photographer, not only should you ask to see his/her work, you should also check references. If possible, talk to vendors the photographer has worked with to see how he/she cooperates with other professionals during the event.

#80 The photographer seems to always be underfoot.

A photographer is hired to capture the special

moments at your events so that you can enjoy the memories over and over again. The best photographers can capture those moments while being discreet. There are those who are always underfoot and in your face. Many times this is because they want to sell as many 8x10s as possible. There has to be a happy compromise between the fun people are having and the pictures taken of them having fun.

Have a conversation with your photographer and talk about the level of intrusion he will have at your event. For example, I have seen very professional photographers who were so concerned about the bride and groom's event that they went out of their way to do most of the "formal" pictures before the event began. Some have taken the "family" photos in as little as 15 minutes while others have taken over an hour. Never permit your photographer to use his/her time as leverage to control yours. The best photographers in the business are there for the entire event. Those that give you limited time may exert pressure on you or your family to do things earlier than your comfort level. Again, talk about these issues before you hire the professional.

#81 I missed some special moments, because I was having my picture taken in the lobby.

Let's use money to make a point. Say a reception costs $25,000, and the event is four hours long. That equates to a little over $100 per minute. If the photographer takes the bride and groom out of their reception to take pictures outside or downstairs to a lobby and that short photo shoot takes 15 minutes, that comes to over $1500 of lost time.

But it's more than that. If a bride and groom are away

for a prolonged period, their guests tend to leave. Guests look to the hosts as the center of attention. If they depart for whatever reason, it's assumed (perhaps subconsciously) that they don't care about their guests. For a little more money, a photographer will take photos hours, days, and even weeks before an event (and certainly afterwards).

Again, let's take a look at the numbers, beginning with a five-hour reception. Some photographers will keep you away from the reception for up to an hour. Add dinner, and soon there are only three hours left. If photos are taken during the event either at an alternate location or perhaps outside at sunset, soon an extra half hour is gone and only two-and-a-half hours remain to enjoy the reception.

One bride and groom were absent from their reception for an hour and a half before the event even started. I stood on the front steps of the venue with the bride's upset parents when the limousine finally came around the corner. It stopped at the base of the hill, and we watched as the bride and groom exited the limo to have a picture taken near a tree. We later discovered that the photographer had the driver pull over and then told the bride and groom that the tree was the ideal place to have a perfect picture taken. Ten minutes later, they got back in the limo and traveled the last hundred yards to the steps of the venue. I received multiple complaints from the guests during the first two hours because of the lack of concern for their wellbeing. On the other hand, the photos taken will last for years to come. The choice is yours.

Another decision to consider is whether it is more important to have a group (family) picture taken center stage and on the dance floor, stopping any and all momentum and fun that is taking place—or to keep the adrenaline and fun flowing by taking the photo session to an alternative location. Again, there are two entirely different viewpoints from two entirely different professionals, but it's the client who needs to determine which is more important.

#82 I'm exhausted. The photographer had me pose a million times.

Again, having lasting memories of your event is important. But having someone stage every moment as if he were taking a model's photo for a magazine can be exhausting. A model's workday is long and tiring. It takes a lot of work to pose, smile, re-adjust, and smile again. Freeze-frame . . . I know, the song is ringing in your head. The best photographers will do a little of both, posed and spontaneous pictures. The one who can capture the moment while in flight is, in my opinion, a true professional. For example, some photographers will ask the bride to "fake" the bouquet toss in order to capture a staged event. Others will do their very best to capture the moment on the fly.

#83 My pictures don't have the warmth I hoped for. / Special moments of all the fun were not captured.

Photographers use two different types of mediums, digital and film. The photographers that use film will sell you the depth and warmth of the pictures, while the digital pros will take ten times more photos and often capture more moments throughout the event. The flash towers can detract from the overall ambiance in the room and can be another obvious distraction with certain media. (A flash tower is a wireless remote flash on top of a tripod stand.) Technology has improved significantly in the digital world, but it still boils down to your personal preference.

Quite often disposable cameras are set on tables to be used by the guests for spontaneous moments. Photo booths are also now very popular and are a lot of fun for the guests.

#84 There was a mistake on the invitations.

It happens. Names are misspelled. The time is wrong. Wrong locations. Wrong colors. Not enough printed. Too many printed. There was a time when each and every invitation was handwritten. Even then, mistakes were made. Do the best you can to prepare for these types of things. Read the invitation over several times. Ask two or three others to read the draft over again to check everything. Consult with someone about the colors and the design. Check the master list of who was naughty and nice before sending them out. (Oops! Wrong celebration. You get the idea.)

#85 The Best Man totally embarrassed us during his toast.

I've seen brides nearly in tears when a less-than-appropriate toast was given. Some toasts seemed more like roasts.

It's strongly recommended that neither the bride, the groom, nor the parents give toasts (unless, of course, the parent is serving as Best Man or Matron of Honor). I've heard fathers toasting their new sons-in-law and berating them for their jobs or saying something else rude or inappropriate. I discourage parents from ever getting on the microphone, unless a suitable announcement is prewritten.

I also discourage the bride or groom from saying anything on the microphone, simply because it only takes one misspoken word to put a damper on the entire reception. One groom insisted on toasting the two most important women in his life—his mother and his lovely bride Jennifer. And then you heard the microphone striking his forehead. His lovely bride was not named Jennifer. Jennifer was one of the bridesmaids. Who knows what caused him to misspeak. It could have been alcohol induced or just a Freudian slip. But it's not something he could rewind and unsay. Keep it simple; keep it elegant.

Occasionally, a father or mother is asked to be a Best Man or Matron of Honor. When that is the case, it's almost a necessity that they give a toast. Some parents are accustomed to having a little fun at the expense of their children. A toast is not a good time to go in that direction. They may have information about the bride and/or groom that no one else knows or should know. For example, it wasn't long ago that I heard a father toasting his son and in his loving way decided to turn the toast into a roast. The word "penis" was used three times. Something like this should never happen.

One groom wanted to toast the three most important women in his life: his mother, his new wife, and the woman who donated a kidney to save his life. This toast went on for over 15 minutes. It was touching, but was inappropriate for a wedding reception. The focus should never have been diverted off the bride.

There are a few rules to a proper toast:

- Remember, it's a toast, not a speech. A toast to a bride and groom should come from the heart and not be read from a computer printout.
- A toast should not embarrass or humiliate anyone.
- It should be short and to the point—maybe 60 to 90 seconds.
- At the end, the individual should complete the toast by asking everyone to raise their glasses and toast the bride and groom.

#86 I forgot the garter and/or "throw" bouquet.

It doesn't seem like much, but it's easy to do. If a bride and or groom forget to bring the garter, make one. Some DJs may have extra garters in their toolkits. Otherwise, use anything you can find to create one, such as rubber bands, flowers, or even ribbon. Forgetting a small item like the garter should not ruin a memory. The same holds true for the bouquet toss. The throw bouquet can be created by plucking individual flowers from the bridesmaids' bouquets. Taking flowers from the centerpieces would also work.

#87 The bouquet and garter toss did not turn out the way I expected.

There is so much significance in the traditions of a wedding reception. Whoever catches the bouquet and garter toss will be the next to marry! It's believed that this tradition began when our country was first being settled. Men would work the fields in the morning and, in the afternoon, folks would gather in groups to witness the wedding. The brides marrying these hardworking men needed something nice to smell since these guys didn't shower before the ceremony, hence the women would carry bouquets. Once married, they would toss the bouquet to the next bride (a sign that they would need it!).

Many brides choose not to do either in the likelihood that they may be embarrassed in front of friends and family. However, if done correctly, the garter and bouquet toss can be very elegant and a memory that lasts forever.

#88 I'm still digging icing out of my nostrils.

Cake cutting is steeped in tradition as well. The tradition dates back to the founding of this nation, when guests brought cupcakes to the wedding reception as a gift to the bridegroom. These cupcakes were placed on a table in a circular pattern until the only way left was to go was up (which is why today's wedding cakes have tiers). The stacks of cupcakes would often fall over, so people began using sugar icing to keep the layers together. But the icing was thick and would harden. It became very difficult for the bride to cut, so the groom would put his hand over hers to assist her—and thus began another tradition.

Tradition also dictated that the bride and groom would be the first to eat from the cake. They would serve each other to symbolize that they would be serving each other for the rest of their lives. But nowhere in tradition is there any mention of a groom smashing cake into a beautiful bride's face, stuffing her nostrils and her hair with frosting. While some guests may find it amusing, the majority do not. The bride and groom should discuss this aspect of the reception and agree beforehand. Do they want the cake cutting ceremony to be romantic and elegant or messy and unattractive? Bear in mind that if they choose the latter, the bride may need to take a break to repair her makeup.

#89 Don't let anyone handcuff you at your reception.

True story: Police sergeant meets and marries police detective. Her boss thought it would be a great idea to put her under arrest at her reception. So, he handcuffed her and led her from table to table to raise "bail." It was clever and amusing . . . at first. Then he sheepishly approached me with a slight problem. He had forgotten the key. Yep, the bride was handcuffed at her own wedding reception. We had a roomful of police officers, but they were off duty. We managed to find some keys, but it took six different keys to finally find one that fit the handcuffs. It was time consuming, frustrating, and the panic level had risen tremendously. The entertainment value had long since passed. Think twice before you try to pull off something "cute" at your reception. It's best to play it safe . . . and traditional.

#90 I knew there might be issues with dancing, and there were . . .

On one occasion, the bride's family did not condone dancing for religious reasons. However, the groom's family loved to dance. Reaching a compromise, we agreed to postpone the dancing until the event was three-quarters through. The moment the announcement was made for the happy couple's first dance, the bride's entire family quietly got up and left the venue. The groom's family remained and had a great time.

It was unfortunate that the bride's family decided not to stay, but the bride and groom had discussed the situation with me, their DJ, in advance, and we were able to work out a plan that satisfied the bride and the groom.

#91 I can't believe my husband rode his Harley into our ceremony.

It's hard to believe someone would insist on riding a motorcycle into a formal setting like a wedding ceremony, but one groom actually did ride his very loud, very shiny Harley into the outdoor tent and up to the arch. He then parked it off to the side and stepped up to await his bride. I was hoping they would mount the cycle and ride off for the recessional, but . . . sigh . . . they didn't.

I also remember a less-than-romantic fellow talking about how he could never keep a woman around. Apparently, when he would bring a new young lady to his home for the first time, she would be greeted by a large Harley parked in the middle of the living room. When asked why he had a motorcycle in his home, he would respond that she was his first love. Nothing like feeling insecure over a bucket of nuts and bolts! Then he would tell her that when he'd brought the Harley into the living room the first time, his now ex-wife had told him to "get it the hell out of the house." His last words to her before she went out the door with her bags were, "That Harley has more chrome than you and certainly is louder than you. It stays."

The point is, it's perfectly fine for a bride and groom to interject something they're jointly passionate about into their ceremony or reception. But it shouldn't be such a focal point that it detracts from the reason for the event. Some things are poignant and/or fun. Like the handcuffs example earlier, other things can get out of hand or come across as absurd or ridiculous. Keep everything in perspective. You don't want to look back at those wedding photos and say, "What were we thinking?" (And have to admit you weren't!)

#92 Everything fell behind schedule because of one little overlooked detail...

There are so many details that must be set in motion for an event of any size to go off without a hitch. And just one detail that you never even thought to put on a to-do list (if you are planning the ceremony or reception on your own, without a professional staff) can muddle it all up. For example, as I arrived to set up my "mini" rig for the ceremony portion of an event, I found dozens of people congregating at the front door of the small chapel. No one had thought of one small detail: someone needed to pick up the keys to the church. This oversight delayed the ceremony by half an hour or so—and then rippled throughout the rest of the event, so that the entire day ran late—all because of a missing key.

Plan well. Make a list of every necessary detail—even those tiny things that seem to be "givens" or "idiotic." You'd be surprised what people forget or just don't think of. Delegate to others and manage, but stay short of being a dreaded "micromanager" (or "bridezilla" of course!).

#93 If you smoke, they will follow.

The bride and groom are the hosts of the wedding reception. Guests look to them as guides to what should happen. If the happy couple is eating, people eat. If they're dancing, folks dance. If either or both the bride and groom smoke, then you'd expect to find them in smoking area several times during the event. Depending on the situation, it could mean a few seconds to minutes away, in addition to the time it actually takes to smoke a cigarette. If they take multiple smoke breaks, the total time can really add up.

Take into consideration that those who smoke also hang out with those who smoke. They will not only follow, they'll remain in a smoking area creating their own party environment. It's not unusual to have to send someone to fetch the wayward guests. It's even sadder to have to remind a bride and groom to return to their own party. Too much time spent outdoors away from the main reception area will most likely cause non-smoking guests to leave early.

As mentioned previously, always consider the financial impact of being absent even for a few minutes from a very expensive event. It's your day of a lifetime—you should spend every moment you can enjoying the spotlight!

#94 I feel old, I feel blue, because there's nothing in my shoe . . .

The saying goes: *Something old, something new, something borrowed, something blue, and a silver sixpence in her shoe.*

Each item in this poem represents a good-luck token for the bride. The tradition is, if she carries them all on her wedding day, her marriage will be happy. "Something old" symbolizes continuity with the bride's family and the past. "Something new" means optimism and hope for the bride's new life ahead. "Something borrowed" is usually an item from a happily married friend or family member whose good fortune in marriage is supposed to carry over to the new bride. The borrowed item also reminds the bride that she can depend on her friends and family.

As for the colorful item, blue has been connected to weddings for centuries. In ancient Rome, brides wore blue to symbolize love, modesty, and fidelity. Christianity has long pictured the Virgin Mary in blue, so purity was associated with the color. Before the late 19th century, blue was a popular color for wedding gowns, as evidenced in proverbs like, "Marry in blue, lover be true."

And finally, a silver sixpence in the bride's shoe represents wealth and financial security. It may date back to a Scottish custom of a groom putting a silver coin under his foot for good luck. For optimum fortune, the sixpence should be in the left shoe. These days, a dime or a copper penny is sometimes substituted, and many companies sell keepsake sixpences for weddings. (Check out the Internet.)

What you don't want is:

Something worn out;

Something so new it hurts;

Something stolen;

Something on your dress

(Oops! It's dessert!)

And the only thing you have left

to your name is your shirt . . .

Okay, maybe I'm not a poet, but you get the idea. A wedding reception, even by tradition, should be a happy time, full of hope and future prosperity. Planning well and using your head should help in making that possible.

Be responsible with your budget. Be moderate with your beverages. Be smart about your comfort. Be aware of your guests and, most of all, remember that it's your day to have fun, not fret about every little thing that may go wrong. Let the little stuff—and some of the big stuff—roll off your shoulders.

What to Wear!

Making it through the
Reception without Screaming

**#95 I had a wedding gown that "screamed"
discomfort.**

Polls tell us that the number one item on any bride's
list of purchases is her wedding dress. The importance of
the look and feel of the dress is paramount in most brides'
eyes. What's interesting is that the dress has absolutely
nothing to do with the success of the reception. On the
other hand, it has everything to do with whether the
reception becomes a nightmare for the bride. Some
complain that it's too tight . . . that's a lot of pain to endure
for a very long day. Some complain that it's too loose.
Again, readjusting a loose garment over and over can
become a nuisance. If it's fragile, the bride spends the
entire day walking on pins and needles. If it's too
expensive, and most are, the concern of getting it dirty is
always on the bride's mind. In some cases, the bustling

becomes a tedious task if prior training is not done.

After seeing thousands of brides in some of the most beautiful bridal dresses—in addition to witnessing the tears from the discomfort and burden of a dysfunctional dress— let me share a little feedback and offer some common sense. Your dress should be comfortable. Not too heavy. Not too big. If it has a train that you're going to "bustle," it should be user-friendly. [Note: Bustling is when you take all that material from the bride's train and "button" it up in the back, creating a bustle of material. This permits the bride to dance and travel around the room without sweeping the floor or needing someone to carry her train.] In my experience, more than half of all bustles *fail*—they fall apart. Almost every dress is different and the method of bustling is at times challenging. The worst-case scenario is that it doesn't work at all. When bustling totally malfunctions, the bride is left holding her train. Again, a tedious task for someone wanting to enjoy her day.

I carry in my bridal toolbox a large cuff to help brides that are at the end of their emotional ropes because their bustles continue to come undone. Brides, insist on having a top-notch bustling system when you purchase your dress. Or hope that *your* DJ has that cuff in his case.

Even more problematic is the weight of the dress. Brides are not used to supporting a garment that is three to six times heavier than any other item in their closets. This puts a serious strain on a bride's energy level. Add the lack of rest and a few beverages, and most wish the day ended sooner than later.

Every so often, a bride purchases a gown that displays her "assets" a little too much. This becomes a concern when the dress gets a mind of its own. Many brides spend an inordinate amount of time pulling up their dresses. With a little research, planning—and trying on several different styles of dresses—one can avoid pain, embarrassment, discomfort, and dysfunction.

Packing up everything you need for a wedding reception can be almost like preparing for a two- or three-day trip. Wearing comfortable clothing (especially shoes!) before the event can help keep the bride relaxed and at ease.

[TIP: While wearing a bridal gown, most brides should seek assistance when visiting the restroom.]

#96 No one knows how to bustle my dress.

One of the duties of the Matron/Maid of Honor is to bustle the bride's dress so she may dance and move around without stepping on or tripping over her train. In my experience, that duty is rarely mastered. Several people in the bridal party should practice this ahead of time. Again, it is not unusual to see a gaggle of people surrounding the bride's train all attempting to figure out the difficult process of bustling the bridal gown. Don't be surprised if the photographer is also among those trying to lend a hand. And don't be surprised if the bustle continues to come undone throughout the evening. I've yet to see a bustle that hasn't come undone at the most inopportune time.

Many Matron/Maids of Honor don't understand the method or the necessity of bustling. This should not be practiced on the wedding day. Those responsible should learn how to bustle the bride's dress days, maybe weeks, in advance, not only ensuring that they know how to bustle the dress, but that the system used will hold and not cause the bride grief during the event.

#97 My feet hurt!

Shoes can be a major source of pain for a bride. Cinderella slippers may be beautiful for the wedding ceremony, but you might not make it through the reception with them. It's strongly recommended that you bring a pair of comfortable (yet beautiful!) slippers along to change into when the heels become a bigger pain than they're worth.

#98 I feel like I'm going to "pop" out of this dress.

Quite often, bridesmaids spend most of the evening looking like they are going to flap their wings and fly. Grasping the top of the dress with both hands, they pull upwards, concerned their strapless gowns are going to slip, exposing more skin than desired. Find a style of dress that will accommodate all of your bridesmaids' tastes and body types.

#99 Most bridesmaids hate their dresses.

They hate the style, the color, and the fact that they have to wear something out of their comfort zone. And they're probably hating the fact that they paid for a dress they'll only get to wear once.

A great way to give the bridesmaids a little leeway is to allow them to accessorize their dresses with jewelry that is complementary to their own personal style. Another great idea is to choose dresses that have two parts, top and bottom, and, at some point during the evening, allow them to remove one or the other for something more comfortable. For example, they can wear the top and put on jeans and cowboy boots. (This would also give you some great variety and fun for your photo booth!)

The colors of bridesmaids' dresses have always been controversial. Why not choose a color you know they would appreciate and wouldn't mind going to a nightclub immediately following your reception. In other words, pick something they wouldn't mind wearing some other time.

#100 What is the entertainer wearing?

It takes a different level of professionalism to have pride in oneself and come dressed appropriately. Weddings typically demand a tux. Not owning one is one thing. Not having one to wear, either borrowed or rented is unacceptable. Ask your band or DJ company if the entertainer(s) will be wearing a tux. There are some circumstances when the bride and groom have other themes or less-than-formal receptions. These are exceptions and should be discussed with the entertainer in advance. Some larger companies may have a uniform shop or partner shop that may have tuxes. It's a good investment for any entertainer who performs in executive-style events or weddings. (A tux is considered a uniform and, if used only for the performance of the job, is a tax deduction. The rule is that if you can wear it to church, then you cannot use it as a tax deduction.).

Would you like your entertainer to be wearing a T-shirt or Hawaiian shirt? There are occasions when this would be appropriate, as your entertainer should never overdress the bridal party. For example, if your bridal party is wearing sports coats and collared shirts, it would be too much for your entertainer to be wearing a tux. It would create an awkward atmosphere and steal the bridal party's thunder. The opposite is also true; if the bridal party is well-dressed (and they usually are), then the entertainer should also be well-dressed, either in a tux or a shirt and tie. On a side note, your entertainer should have good personal hygiene and ensure that the tux or shirt-and-tie outfit is well pressed and clean.

The entertainer should not be seen setting up his equipment wearing the same outfit he plans to be wearing during your event. That is completely unprofessional. While he can set up equipment and do sound checks wearing jeans or whatever is comfortable, he should change into acceptable wedding attire before the guests arrive and the event begins.

Some brides choose to have theme receptions, such as Country or Hawaiian. Ensure your entertainer is aware of your theme, and ask if they can dress appropriately. In most cases, they'll be glad to do so.

#101 Many of our guests were not dressed appropriately for a formal function.

As the guests were arriving, slowly but surely it was obvious that there was an issue with the clothing they had chosen. I was directed to look at the top of the wedding cake. Hmm. It seems a Pittsburgh Steelers fan was now married to a Green Bay Packers fan—and the top of the cake sported both Steelers and Packers helmets! I was then told that the guests were asked to come dressed in the colors of their teams. So half of the guests were dressed in green and yellow, and the other half were dressed in silver and black. It looked more like a Halloween party than a wedding reception!

It all boils down to "be careful what you ask for." A

wedding reception is a formal event in most cases. Having a theme is fine, as long as it doesn't turn your event into a circus. Even if you and your husband are fun and quirky and want a unique, memorable event, your guests and family should not be leaving your event checking their shoes for foreign matter or examining their hair for ticks. Include your personalities into your event, but keep it respectable and enjoyable for all.

Afterword

When one Mother of the Bride approached me on a rainy wedding day and told me, "I've heard if something doesn't go wrong at a wedding, it's bad luck for the bride and groom," I responded by telling her how bad I felt. She looked at me with a puzzled expression. I explained that if what she said was true, then I was the cause of dooming countless couples to years of misfortune. If they'd read this book and heeded its advice—based on my years of experience—then they'd made good decisions, enjoyed lovely, smooth-flowing wedding receptions . . . and avoided those "somethings" going wrong.

Hundreds of decisions have to be made in planning this event of a lifetime. One thing is for certain, the day will definitely be memorable. Will that day be a dream come true—or a nightmare? It's depends primarily on the planning. My wish is that this book will help brides and grooms make lasting, beautiful memories and, hopefully, avoid those mishaps that make that special day less than picture perfect.

About the Author

Rex De Jaager, "The Rexpert," is retired from the U.S. Navy and confesses that his friends and family thought he had lost his mind when he gave up a great second career as a high school teacher to open up an entertainment business. He admits he'd much rather be at a party or reception than act as referee at a perpetual spitball fight. After all, parties are full of fun, laughter, and—when he has anything to say about it—great music.

In his 25 years of experience as Disc Jockey and Master of Ceremonies, Rex has witnessed hundreds of situations where he wished the bride and/or groom had been given some sage advice to be able to avoid catastrophes. De Jaager doles out that wisdom in *101 Ways to Screw Up Your Wedding Reception (Without Really Trying)*. It is his intention to guide couples towards a hassle-free, successful, and sweetly memorable day of their dreams.

Made in the USA
Lexington, KY
22 February 2013